DISCLAIMER: This book, entitled *Heaven and Hell*, is not to be confused with the Meat Loaf album by the same name,* released in 1993. Meat Loaf did not write this book and any similarities between the two works are mere coincidence. For a more complete discography of Meat Loaf (aka Marvin Lee Aday), as it relates to the themes of heaven and hell, please turn to page 124.

*Or, for that matter, the Black Sabbath album *Heaven and Hell*, released in 1980.

Heaven and Hell, unknown German master

HEAVEN

AND

HELL

A Compulsively Readable Compendium
of Myth, Legend, Wisdom, and Wit
for Saints and Sinners

MARA FAUSTINO

Atlantic Monthly Press
New York

Published simultaneously in Canada
Printed in the United States of America

Every effort has been made by the author to secure permissions from all copyright holders. Any errors or omissions brought to the publisher's attention will be corrected in future editions.

FIRST EDITION

Library of Congress Cataloging-in-Publication Data

Faustino, Mara.

    Heaven and hell : a compulsively readable compendium of myth, legend, wisdom, and wit for saints and sinners / Mara Faustino.
       p. cm.
     ISBN 0-87113-696-1
     1. Heaven.   2. Hell.   I. Title.

  BL540.F38 2004
  202'.3—dc22   2004050203

Atlantic Monthly Press
an imprint of Grove/Atlantic, Inc.
841 Broadway
New York, NY 10003

04 05 06 07 08   10 9 8 7 6 5 4 3 2 1

CONTENTS

Contents

Contents

LIST OF ILLUSTRATIONS

FAUSTINO'S INDEX

Number of hot hells, according to Buddhism: 8

Number of cold hells, according to Buddhism: 8

Number of Muhammadan heavens: 7

Number of angel orders, according to the Pseudo-Dionysius Hierarchy: 9

Number of demonic orders, according to the Pseudo-Dionysius Hierarchy: 9

Number of heavens shown to Enoch (later Metatron): 10

Number of rivers in hell: 5

Number of bars with "hell" in the title in New York City: 1

Number of miles from Prosper, Michigan, to Hell, Michigan: 171.42

Number of pairs of wings the angel Metatron possesses: 32

Number of destinies into which one may be reincarnated, according to Buddhism: 6

Number of figures said to have ascended to Heaven in the Bible: 5

Number of patron angels protecting nations: 70

Number of acres that make up Hell Hole Bay Wilderness: 2,125

Ratio of songs about angels to songs not about angels in 1990: 1:10

Number of wings an angel in the Seraphim order has: 6

Number of doors in Valhalla: 540

Number of items in a devil's dozen: 13

Duration of the universe's cycle according to Hinduism: 30,000 years

Number of angels in heaven, according to Daniel's vision: 100 million

Number of angels created on the second day of creation, according to the kabbalah: 600 million

Number of angels that exist, according to the Jewish scholar Simon ben Lakish (third century): 1.06434 quintillion

Number of angels that exist, according to medieval scholars: 301,655,722 (with 133,306,608 of those angels as fallen)

Number of cherubim created by Michael, according to the Koran: 700 quadrillion

HEAVEN

Etymologically, the origins of *heaven* are unclear. Linguists trace the word back to the German words *himil* or *himin*, which might come from the word *home*, as in "the home of God." Another, equally plausible possibility is that *heaven* derives from *ham*, "to cover." This latter definition may be responsible for the concept of heaven as the "roof of the world." In Hebrew, "heaven" is plural, though it is usually translated into the singular form. Biblically, *heaven* is used to describe both a physical place as part of the universe and also God's dwelling place. Many religions possess variations of the Christian heaven, maintaining the idea of a joyful afterlife somewhere in the religion's cosmography. According to the Talmud, one hour of bliss in Heaven is equivalent to the collective bliss one has experienced in his/her entire life.

Heaven

Dutch	*paradijs*	Japanese	*tengoku*
French	*ciel*	Portuguese	*céu*
	Spanish	*cielo*	

HEAVEN ALTERNATIVES

1. PARADISE: 1. Formally, the word is used to describe the blissful place for the just, before they receive their judgment. 2. Informally, it now means a perfect place, blissful. 3. Also an architectural term to denote a closed-in atrium at one side of the church (west). 4. Place described by Joni Mitchell in song "Big Yellow Taxi" (now paved, and containing a parking lot). Also in this former paradise (according to Mitchell): a pink hotel, a boutique, and a "swinging hot spot." 4. Milton's epic poems *Paradise Lost* and *Paradise Regained* (the sequel to *Lost*) have also explored paradise, as a concept. 5. Other literary explorations of and references to paradise: *This Side of Paradise* by F. Scott Fitzgerald (1920) and William Morris's *The Earthly Paradise* (1868–1870), told in Chaucerian meter. 6. Ridvan, which translates into "paradise," is a spot outside of Baghdad,

recognized by followers of the Bahai faith as a particularly holy place. 7. Bird of paradise is a name used to describe both a species of bird (New Guinea, Australia) as well as a kind of flower (also called *strelitzia*).

2. NIRVANA: 1. A Buddhist concept referring to the goal of the Buddhist eightfold path. In Buddhism, two different notions of Nirvana are distinguished: "Nirvana with a remainder" and "Nirvana without a remainder." The former connotes a state of enlightenment and bliss that occurs during life, whereas the latter connotes the same state of bliss and freedom, but as it occurs after death. Though the concept is complex, the term is now popularly used to describe a sense of enlightenment as well as freedom from petty constraints and bother. 2. A post-punk band led by Kurt Cobain, which not only defined the grunge movement but also launched the Seattle-based indie record label Sub Pop, releasing the label's first album (*Bleach*). The band was founded in 1987 but rose to MTV-sized fame when it released *Nevermind* in 1991, which hit number 1 on the Billboard chart by January 1992. "Smells Like Teen Spirit" became an anthem for a generation of fans. In 1994 Cobain was found dead of a self-inflicted shotgun wound and it was ruled a suicide. His notebooks were released in 2002. Neil Young released a tribute album to Cobain titled *Sleep With Angels*.

3. VALHALLA: According to Norse mythology, Valhalla is a lavish hall where Odin receives the souls of slain heroes—think Viking heaven. A wolf guards the western door, one of 540 doors in total.

4. GAN EDEN: This is not the same as the Garden of Eden, where Adam and Eve resided. *Gan Eden*, a Hebrew name, is the place for those who achieve spiritual perfection, and only a very small fraction of those who die travel directly to *Gan Eden*. According to the Jewish concept of *Gan Eden*, some people may ultimately reside in *Gan Eden* after going through a purification process. These processes would happen in a place of punishment, such as Gehenna (*see Gehenna, page 6*). *Gan Eden* is portrayed as a peaceful place, containing about sixty times the joy one might experience on Shabbat.

5. AVALON: A mythic place of Arthurian times, the Isle of Avalon is said to be the place where King Arthur went after disappearing. Avalon

was home to one of the underworld gods, Afallach, though the myth allows that King Arthur journeyed there to heal his battle wounds.

"From Avalon" by Emily Huntington Miller

I know it well, that green and tranquil isle,
Encircled by the arms of summer tides
That sway and smile, and whisper of the sea.
Not far away it lies; its fragrant shades
Shot through by golden lances of the sun,
And stirred by gentle airs that wander still
On noiseless feet, to find the chamber fair
Where, couched on mystic herbs and asphodel,
Healed of his hurts, King Arthur lies asleep.
Oft have I found its shelter. When the stress
Of warring winds, and sharp tumultuous storms
Have left me spent and breathless on the field,
Then my swift thoughts, for healing and for rest,
Bear me away to peaceful Avalon.

6. ISLAND OF THE BLEST: Considered a more blissful destination even than Elysian fields (see below), the Island of the Blest is the ultimate fate of those good souls who persevere three times against sin, or (in an alternate interpretation) for those good souls who pass through three lifetimes.

See "The Three-Decker" on page 96.

7. ELYSIAN FIELDS: The part of Hades most reminiscent of heaven, according to Greek mythology.

8. AMARAVATI: The capital of Svarga, and also a temporary paradise for the dead. Ruled by Indra.

9. MAG MELL: "Plain of Joy," according to Celtic mythology; also called Tir na n-Og, or "land of youth." Visualized as both an island and a place at the bottom of the sea, Mag Mell was ruled by King Tethra.

10. TUONELA: The peaceful place of death for innocent people as well as children. Tuonela is part of a larger realm of the dead, called Manala, according to Finnish mythology.

11. BUROKU: According to Polynesian mythology, the dead are divided in the following way: a very few of the lucky ones are taken to Buroku,

or heaven, and the rest are thrown into a lake, where they eventually sink and meet various punishments, according to their lives.

12. FLAITHINIS: According to Celtic mythology, the term "Flaithinis" is used to acknowledge "heaven" as a Christian concept. Flaithinis is regarded as a semi-imaginary island in the West.

13. SUKHAVATI ("Pure Land"): Considered the "Western Paradise" in Buddhism.

14. PARADISE GARDEN: Actually, Paradise Garden is an elaborate work of folk art on this earth, in Pennville, Georgia, specifically. Constructed by artist Howard Finster, Paradise Garden is a massive installation that occupies a two-and-a-half-acre piece of swampland. Constructed primarily of refuse, this environmental Eden is filled with a rusted bicycle tower, an eight-foot concrete shoe, and walkways made of mirror fragments.

15. AALU: Part of the Egyptian concept of the afterlife, Aalu is the place for "good" people, a paradise ruled by Osiris. The Fields of Aalu are filled with the friends and family of the deceased, and these people rise up to greet the new arrival. Though the landscape of Aalu was imagined as beautiful, inhabitants of Aalu still had to work the land. Some Egyptians were once buried with tools in their tombs for this purpose.

See terms for heaven in the Bible, page 31

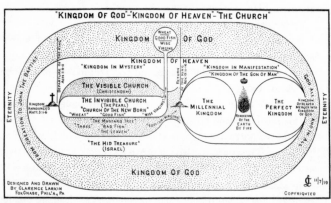

The Heavens, Clarence Larkin

HELL

Etymologically, the word *hell* may come from the words *hole* and *hollow*, to indicate a dark, cavernous place, or from *helian* or *behelian*, which means "to hide." Ultimately, hell was and continues to be depicted as a dark, hidden place made of fire and unpleasantness. In Norse mythology, *hel* is the goddess of the underworld. Hell, in English, corresponds to the Latin *infernus*; the Greek *hades*; and the Hebrew *sheol*.

Hell

Dutch	*hel*	Indonesian	*neraka*
Finnish	*helvetti*	Italian	*inferno*
French	*enfer*	Czech	*peklo*
German	*hölle*	Danish	*helvede*

HELL ALTERNATIVES

1. HADES: According to Greek mythology, Hades is the god of the underworld, also known as "the Lord of the Dead," "the Rich One" (he lives among precious minerals from the earth), the "Hospitable One" (somewhat facetious—he accepts anyone and everyone), and as brother of Zeus. Hades kidnapped the goddess Persephone (also known as the "ice queen") and brought her to the underworld. Hades was an unpopular god among the other Greek gods and goddesses, and rarely let anyone out of Hades, with a few exceptions. Ultimately, Hades's domain of the underworld or netherworld became known as "Hades," too.

2. TARTARUS: According to Greek mythology, Tartarus is even lower than Hades. It's described as a dark pit encircled by a bronze wall, encased by three layers of night.

3. NIFLHEIM: According to Norse mythology, Niflheim is a cold and dark place at the lowest level of the world. It's located under the third root of Yggdrasil, the great ash tree whose stem supports the earth, while its branches overshadow the world and reach up beyond the heavens.

4. SHE'OL: a synonym for Gehenna. See Gehenna, below.

5. UCA PACHA: According to Incan mythology, Uca Pacha is an underworld located at the center of the earth and is similar to hell.

6. TOPHET: a place near Jerusalem, in the valley of Hinnom. In the Bible, the word becomes a synonym for Hell.

7. GEHENNA: A Yiddish word, synonymous with Gehinnom (Hebrew), also sometimes called She'ol. Gehenna has been compared to the Christian concept of hell (fire and brimstone), though most see Gehenna as a place and time when Jews who have passed from mortal life can view and objectively examine their past actions and the consequences of those actions. One belief states that every time a Jewish person "sins," s/he creates an angel of destruction, and these angels of destruction would potentially face their creators (sinners) in the afterlife. Gehenna, however, is not a permanent residing place; those who pass through are held no longer than twelve months before taking their places in the afterlife, or (in Hebrew) Olam Ha-Ba. A very few—the most evil—do not move on, but the Jewish tradition encompasses multiple interpretations on what, exactly, happens to these souls.

8. YOMI-NO-KUNI: According to those who believe in Shinto, Yomi-no-kuni is an underworld in which grotesque beasts guard the exits. Similar to Buddhist interpretations of "hell" or the underworld, this place is not permanent but is, instead, a place for those sent here to "repent" or cleanse themselves of "sin" before exiting this realm.

9. AMENTI: According to Ancient Egyptian cosmology, Amenti is the place where Osiris, the king of the underworld, judges souls, relegating them for punishment or reward. *See "The weighing of the heart in the Hall of Truth," page 83.*

10. AL-NAR, or JAHANNAM: This place is described in the Koran as a place of crackling fire and dark smoke, with seven gates. Each gate represents a level. Those Muslims who stray from the faith and/or commit sins end up here. Those who try to escape are dragged back with hot, iron hooks.

11. NARAKA: The Buddhist underworld, and also the name of a Hindu goddess.

12. XIBALBA: In Mayan mythology, Xibalba is an underworld situated at the end of a long, thorny road, filled with danger, and ruled by

Hun Came and Vucub Caquix (also the father of two demonic giants, Cabrakan and Zipacna). The *Popol Vuh* is one of the best-known documents of Mayan mythology.

13. METNAL: In Mayan mythology, Metnal is the worst of the nine hells and is ruled by Ah Puch (see Xibalba, above).

See terms for hell in the Bible, page 68.

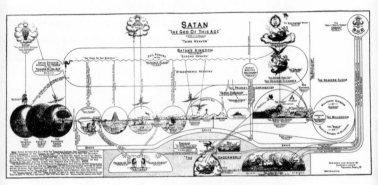

The Underworld, Clarence Larkin. Clarence Larkin was born in 1850 in Pennsylvania and was employed in a bank before working as a mechanical engineer and professional draftsman. Ultimately he became a teacher for the blind as well as an American Baptist pastor. He drew more than a hundred meticulous charts before he died in 1924.

See other Larkin images, pages 4, 64, 113.

BETWEEN PLACES: PURGATORY

1. PURGATORY: Viewed as the final purification by Catholics, purgatory is a place for those with "small sins" to prepare for heaven. The length and severity of time in purgatory is in accordance with the deceased's sin(s).

2. LIMBO: Not a bat mitzvah party game, this is actually a place where the righteous waited, before Christ opened the gates to Heaven. The term is also used loosely to describe the place for those souls who

are both too good to go to hell but too bad to go to heaven. Similar to purgatory, limbo is considered more of a place rather than a phase or stage.

3. BARZAKH: A place of waiting, according to the Muslim faith. A dead person waits here until the Day of Judgment.

4. ADLIVUN: According to Inuit mythology, this underworld is beneath the land and above the sea—a place for the deceased to purify themselves before traveling to the Land of the Moon, described as restful and peaceful. Though Adlivun is a frozen wasteland, in terms of landscape, it prepares souls who pause there for the next stop.

LIMBO CHOW: EGGS IN PURGATORY

Ingredients:

3 tablespoons olive oil
4 cloves garlic, minced
7 fresh large tomatoes, skin and seeds
  removed, cut up
Fresh parsley, minced
Fresh basil, minced
Salt and black pepper to taste
3 jalapeño or serrano peppers, chopped
8 eggs

1. Put olive oil into a large frying pan. Sauté garlic until golden brown.
2. Add tomatoes, parsley, basil, peppers, plus salt and pepper to the skillet. Cook about 45 minutes.
3. Break the eggs into a side dish without breaking yolks and then slide them into the frying pan. Cover the pan with a lid and simmer slowly until the eggs are cooked.
   Serves 4.

See Cookbook: Noshing in Nirvana, Snacking with Satan, page 114

ANGELS

Etymologically, the word comes from the Latin *angelus* and the Greek *Angelos*, meaning "messenger." The biblical name for angel was *mal'akh*. Although angels have supernatural powers, they often appear in human form, according to the Bible. Angels are assigned to special missions, acting in various capacities, such as messengers or interpreters, and are considered to be the conduits of God's power. Though pop culture insists upon the image of a cherublike angel as a symbol, less innocent, fallen angels do exist. According to the Koran, the number of wings an angel has may vary, ranging from two to four. In new age religions, angels are sometimes referred to as *dakini*. Informally, a financial backer of a business scheme or political campaign is called an angel.

Angel

Finnish	*enkeli*	Italian	*angelo*
French	*ange*	Latin	*angelus*
German	*engel*	Portuguese	*anjo*
Indonesian	*malaikat*	Spanish	*ángel*

THE NINE ORDERS OF ANGELS

[According to the Pseudo-Dionysius Hierarchy of Angels]

First Choir:

1. SERAPHIM: These angels are closest to the throne of God. They are too bright with love to be looked upon by other divine beings; their light is too intense. They can also be found chanting

"Holy, holy, holy..." (the Trisagion), encircling God's throne. Only four angels are in this highest section of the angel hierarchy. In the Book of Revelation, these same angels are described as "four holy beasts," with four faces and six wings.

2. CHERUBIM: These angels hold the knowledge of God, and are also responsible for both guarding the stars and traveling to earth for the heavy tasks (such as expelling man from the Garden of Eden). Before his fall, Satan was a cherub. They are the first angels mentioned in the Old Testament. Though depicted as fat, winged babies on stickers, T-shirts, and greeting cards, cherubs were actually described as sphinxlike creatures and were depicted in ancient Assyrian art as winged creatures with human faces but with bodies like eagles, bulls, or sphinxes.

3. THRONES (or Ophanim): These angels make up God's chariot. Oddly enough, they are described as large wheels, covered with eyes, glowing with light. They are sometimes called "wheels," for short (should you ever have a need to call out).

Second Choir:

1. DOMINIONS: These angels are "the managers." They mediate the orders from the upper choir and pass them on to the lower choir, not an entirely bad situation. More difficult, however, is their charge to maintain the order of the cosmos. They hold a scepter and rarely make themselves known to mortals.

2. VIRTUES: These angels deal with the natural world, presiding over weather as well as the material world, in which they must bestow material blessings upon God's favorites.

3. POWERS: These angels are on border patrol, carefully maintaining the border between heaven and earth. They watch over mortals leaving earth to make sure they reach heaven. Historically, this order of angels has the most fallen angels.

Third Choir:

1. PRINCIPALITIES: These angels watch over humans directly, protecting cities and towns on earth. They carry out orders from higher angels and manage the duties of lower angels.

10

2. ARCHANGELS: A confusing category, the archangels are not to be confused with the terms as applied to the highest angels. They are the category directly above the order Angels. Their duties include watching over the Angels and leading the divine army during battles.

3. ANGELS: This group is closest to earth. Angels watch locally over households and specific people, as opposed to those higher orders that watch over entire nations. They carry God's words to humans, acting as messengers and guides. The Hebrew word for Angel (*mal'akh*) translates as "messenger," while the Persian word for Angel (*angaros*) translates as "courier."

See Nine Orders of Demons on page 81

ANGELIC SEALS

Used to call the spirits of the angels, these seals have been largely co-opted by those interested in the occult. These seals can be found in both the Greater Key of Solomon and the Lesser Key of Solomon.

INS AND OUTS OF HEAVEN AND HELL

Heaven

In	Out
1. Halos, see *Wings*	1. High ponytails: inconvenient
2. Wings: very "Club Kid NYC," see *Halos*	2. Backpacks: like high ponytails, these prove impractical
3. Pastels: think "Cruisewear"	3. Gold lamé
4. Long, white robes: classic	4. Bathrobes (Would you kiss God in that *shmata*?!)
5. Rouge, color gel	5. Powder blush
6. Autoharp	6. Classic harp
7. Bare feet	7. Hiding your feet under your long robe
8. Pedicures (see above, no. 7)	8. Perms
9. Figure eights (flight pattern)	9. Nosedives
10. Privacy	10. Watching over people
11. Lactose-free/ Soy milk miracles	11. Miracles involving milk-drinking statues

See Miracles, page 13

Hell

In	Out
1. Horns: classic	1. Goatee: Passé
2. Tails: from the ass	2. Tails/Mullets: from the head
3. Bikinis	3. Tankinis
4. Lightning	4. Pyrotechnics
5. Speakeasies	5. Caves
6. Personal assistants	6. Sidekicks
7. Boule	7. Darts
8. Carmine, or cerise	8. The color red
9. Mischief	9. Evil
10. Stocks	10. Bonds

MIRACLES

1. THE SADDENED STATUE: Originally made by Jose Thedim in 1946, a second International Pilgrim Virgin Statue was made and blessed in 1947. The two statues were scheduled to travel the world until they reached Russia. The Pope (Pius XII) even blessed the first statue in 1946. In 1972, the statue was brought to the New Orleans diocese, where it reportedly began to shed tears upon "numerous occasions." The tears, it's claimed, are human tears and though not everyone can see them they cause a dry cloth to become damp. See the Bleeding Statue, below.

2. MARY'S MONEY-MARKETING WATCH: In 1996, an apparition of Mary appeared on the side of the Seminole Finance Building in Clearwater, Florida, in the form of colorful streaks spread over a dozen glass panes. More than 1.5 million people came to visit when it appeared and remained for approximately three weeks, over Christmas. The colorful streaks were like those made by mineral streaks, sometimes caused when a building is hit with water from a sprinkler or rain. People traveled to the Finance Building with candles, flowers, and stuffed animals, and reportedly wept, prayed, and fainted after viewing the saint-in-streaks. One receptionist in the building at the time said, "It's very spiritual, very peaceful." In 1997 a vandal threw liquid at the apparition and disturbed it. Several thunderstorms later, however, she reappeared. The Clearwater City Council had to make provisions for new pedestrian and vehicle traffic.

3. BLEEDING STATUE: As reported in the *Guardian*, December 4, 1992, a six-inch porcelain statue, belonging to a housewife in a working-class district of Santiago, wept tears of blood. The coroner's office in Santiago tested the blood and determined it was human blood, type O. The statue is reported to cry more fervently around children. Supposedly, scientists CAT-scanned the statue. (Were they

looking for a brain, too? Isn't it enough that the statue cries?) Reportedly, weeping statues have been found in Australia (1994), Benin (1997), Ireland (1994–95), Mexico (1992), Puerto Rico (1994), Spain (1998), Trinidad (1996), Las Vegas (1998), Kansas (1996), Virginia (1992), and Italy (on four different occasions).

4. THE MAMMARIAN MIRACLE: On September 21, 1995, thousands of milk-drinking Hindu statues drank greedily from spoons of the devout. All over India, the police tried to control crowds who were pushing into temples with jugs, saucepans, clay pots, and cups of milk. As one person wisely put it, "It cannot be a hoax. Where would all the milk go?" Based on varied accounts, this dairy frenzy lasted twenty-four hours or one month.

5. THE ALLAH AUBERGINE (and Watermelon): On January 20, 1996, shortly before Ramadan, a farmer in Senegal discovered a watermelon on which the name "Allah" appeared. Similarly, a woman in England sliced open an eggplant to discover the seeds in the perfect arrangement of the Muslim "Ya-Allah," which means "Allah exists." Apparently, this was not the only time Allah reminded people to eat their fruits and vegetables. After the '96 watermelon, and the '97 aubergine, a miraculous tomato appeared in Huddersfield, Britain, along with two simultaneous "aubergine miracles" in Great Britain in 1997, and yet another on Easter Monday in 1998.

6. CRYING CRYSTAL: From March through November 1996, a twelve-year-old Lebanese girl cried tiny crystals. Though the crystals were razor sharp, the girl felt no pain when she cried them. Needless to say, doctors were baffled. And, presumably, Lalique was pounding down her door.

7. ANGELS OF RUST: When a woman's mother was moved into a hospice ward for a brain aneurysm, the daughter was concerned, until she looked out the room's window to see two angels made from rust on top of the air-conditioning units. She knew her mother would be okay (though the same may not be said for the AC unit).

8. THE SACRED SLICK: Though most people would find it merely inconvenient and slippery, the Reverend Moueen Hana of California recognized a miracle in 1995 when his hands filled with olive oil after praying. His icons also oozed olive oil. He traced this miracle

back to a woman in Syria, whose hands also filled with olive oil in 1982, and her icons reportedly seeped fifty-seven gallons of olive oil. That's a religious slick, if not schtick, to be sure!

9. KILIM KRIER: Competing with the novelty of the crystal crier, a young girl in Algeria apparently cried tears of "small, colorful threads." Reported in 1997, it's unclear how long the miracle lasted and whether she made a kilim or left the threads in their pure, unadulterated state.

10. CHRIST ON A ROSE PETAL: A slightly more "rosy" picture than Christ on a cross.

11. "T" TREE: Very simply, a tree in the shape of a cross grew at the Solovki Monastery, in Russia. By Solovki standards, the tree-cross was a miracle.

THE DEVIL, AN INTRODUCTION

Though most popular images portray the devil as a red man with hoofed feet, horns, a tail, a goatee, and sometimes a pitchfork, Grimms' folktales convey an altogether different interpretation of the devil: a Pan-like wood spirit with a penchant for music, who lives with his grandmother. The word *devil* is derived from the Greek word *diabolos*, which means "to slander." However, *devil* is also derived from an Indo-European word, *deva*, which means "angel." Various conceptions of the devil differ and even contradict one another. The Bible does not clarify precisely why Satan, or the devil, was exiled from heaven. In the Muslim version of the Christian story, the devil, or Iblis, is cast out for loving God *too* much; he refuses to bow down to humans.

NICKNAMES FOR THE DEVIL
(Names You Don't Want to Hear on the Playground)

1. PRINCE OF DARKNESS: coined in Milton's *Paradise Lost*.
2. FALLEN ANGEL: coined in Milton's *Paradise Lost*.
3. DIABOLOS: Satan is called *diabolos* thirty-three times in the New Testament.
4. DICKENS: This word is unrelated to Charles Dickens, and might be derived from "devilkins." Shakespeare used the term, and people today use the term in expressions such as "it hurts like the Dickens."
5. OLD ROGER: eighteenth-century nickname.
6. BEELZEBUB: originally a deity named Baal-zebul. In the New Testament (Luke), Satan is compared to Beelzebub, and eventually the two names became synonymous.
7. SATAN: In Hebrew, the devil is called Satan. The Hebrew "Satan" roughly translates to "adversary" or "obstacle." In the Book of Job, Satan appears as an angel. Satan was later exiled by God to "hell," a concept that didn't exist in earlier Jewish tradition but was adopted from Christianity.
8. LUCIFER: a Latin translation of "Morning Star," or the planet Venus. This name was actually a result of imperfect (spotty) exegesis in translation from the cuneiform text.
9. MEPHISTOPHELES: This name comes from the folklore tradition rather than from Christian demonology. It actually appeared during the Renaissance, and appears in the tale of Faustus.
10. PRINCE OF THIS WORLD: Satan is called this in the Book of John (12:31, 14:30).
11. THE BEAST: from the Book of Revelation.
12. THE DRAGON: a name also found in Revelation (12:9).
13. THE EVIL ONE: from the tradition of Christian demonology.
14. THE TEMPTER: from the Book of Matthew.
15. ANTICHRIST: This name stands in for "Devil" in the Book of Revelation. Also used now to describe someone who epitomizes evil.
16. EL DIABLO OR SATANAS: El Diablo comes from the word *diabolos*.

17. SAMUEL: In the kabbalah, Satan is sometimes referred to as Samuel.
18. IBLIS: In Islam, Satan is referred to as Iblis.

Others:

Old Scratch • Old Split-Foot • Der Teufel • The Accuser
The Adversary • The Slandered • The Demon • The Spoiler
The Enemy, Prince of the Power of the Air • That Old Serpent
Belial • The Prince of Pandemonium
Leonard (France, Germany, Switzerland) • Pocker
Old Gooseberry • Old Harry • Old Nick • Mr. Sam
Old Horney

See the Luciferian Lexicon on page 60

A COCKTAIL BREAK:
THREE ANGELIC APERITIFS

Note: All three cocktails are pousse-cafés, meaning: layered drinks. Pour in
the order given, so the heaviest liquors sink to the bottom, and slowly pour
each liquor over a bar spoon handle or a regular spoon.

Angel's Delight

1 part Grenadine
1 part triple sec
1 part Crème Yvette
1 part cream

Angel's Kiss

1 part white crème de cacao
1 part Crème Yvette
1 part five-star brandy
1 part cream

Angel's Tip

1 part brown crème de cacao
1 part cream
(Add a cherry through a toothpick on
   the side)

THINGS THAT COME FROM HEAVEN

1. WEATHER: Queen sang it best ("Made in Heaven").
2. GEORGE BURNS: In *Oh, God!* (1977), George Burns, as God, descends from heaven to find the perfect messenger—a supermarket clerk, played by John Denver, of course. God, as portrayed by Burns, came back "down" for *Oh, God! Book II* in 1980 and *Oh, God! You Devil* in 1984.
3. TEEN ANGELS: The song "Teen Angel," as sung by Mark Dinning, was a million-seller in 1960. Words and music by Jean and Red Surrey
4. BREAD, OR ANGEL BREAD: *see page 56.*
5. MISTLETOE: The druids believed that mistletoe fell from heaven and attached itself to a tree on earth, where it continued to grow, representing the union of heaven and earth and also God's reconciliation with humankind. Likewise, kissing under the mistletoe became a sign of reconciliation and acceptance.
6. SAINTS: *see page 158.*
7. BEES: In both Ireland and Wales, bees are believed to come from heaven and bring secret wisdom with them.
8. STAGS: According to both Celtic and Irish tradition, stags are considered horned gods and act as guides to heaven.

THE ANOREXIC ANGEL?

Suffice to say, angels don't eat. Though angels make occasional appearances at meals with mere mortals, they are merely mimicking the motions, so as to hide their identities (in some cases). Think Genesis 18, when Abraham was visited by three angels disguised as mortals;

God provided these angels with the pretense of noshing though they're actually addicted only to manna (*see angel food, page 114*). Other things that distinguish angels from mortals include celibacy, special languages, supernatural physical strength, and the ability to both fly and transcend time.

SPELLS WITH DEVIL CANDLES
(The Wiccan with a Wick)

DEVIL CANDLES: Those candles sold in voodoo and occult stores can be put to good use.

      Red Devil candles = for spells of sexual domination
    Black Devil candles = to cause harm to an enemy
   Green Devil candles = to receive money owed, or to make easy money. See Money-Back Spell, below.

Money-Back Spell with a Devil Candle

Acquire a Green Devil candle.

Carve the debtor's name into the candle.

On a piece of blank paper, write the debtor's name nine times, and then write across each printed name the words "give me my money."

Put the paper underneath a plate or saucer, on top of which sits the candle.

As you light the candle, recite:

        Green Devil, this is my command:
        Until [name] repays the debt
        Compel him/her to feel the sting of his/her conscience
        Compel him/her to burn with the fire of remorse
        Compel him/her to taste in his/her mouth only ashes
        Compel him/her to dream of the evil s/he's done
        Compel him/her to remember his/her debt to me

> Whenever s/he thinks of money
> Whenever s/he hears the word "money"
> Whenever s/he sees money
> Whenever s/he touches money
> Now give me the money you owe me, [name]
> Or it will be hot for you!

Burn the paper slightly.

Do this for seven days (but don't forget to use the telephone, too).

When debt is repaid, make sure to thank the Green Devil.

A BRIEF HISTORY AND TIME LINE OF THE HELLS ANGELS MOTORCYCLE CLUB

The Hells Angels Motorcycle Club (or HAMC) was officially founded in Fontana, California, in 1948, when Otto Friedli broke off from another motorcycle club called the Pissed Off Bastards to start a new club. The HAMC took its name from an elite division of paratroopers in the U.S. Army's 11th Airborne Division who, during the Second World War, parachuted out of planes with TNT tucked in their pant legs. By some accounts, these Hells Angel vets came home with excess adrenaline, ultimately seeking solace on the open road, on motorcycles. The noisy bikes were cheap in the 1940s, considered war surplus. Other historians say the name was merely a tribute to the 11th Airborne Division, and that the HAMC involved only one member of the original division, Avrid Olsen. Purportedly, Olsen gave the idea for the name to Friedli. Today, chapters of the HAMC exist all over the world (see below). The Hells Angels maintain a varied reputation as both a brotherlike clan running charitable events while riding across the country and as violent outlaws, forming their own version of a Mafia crime ring. As of January 2004, there are 231 HAMC chapters in more than twenty-eight countries.

Heaven and Hell

Some of the Countries with
Hells Angels Motorcycle Club Chapters

Denmark • Holland • Greece • Germany • USA • Italy
Canada • Switzerland • Brazil • Liechtenstein • Argentina
Austria • Australia • England/Wales • South Africa • Finland
Spain • Norway • France • Sweden • New Zealand
Bohemia/Czech Republic • Belgium • Portugal

"Prospects and Hangouts"
for Hells Angels Motorcycle Clubs

Chile • Russia • Croatia

A Time Line

1947: At an American Motorcycle Association convention in Hollister, California, several motorcycle clubs, including the Pissed Off Bastards (POBs) and the Booze Fighters, were drunk and disorderly.

1948: Otto Friedli, of the POBs, broke off and formed the first Hells Angels Motorcycle Club in Fontana, California.

1954: The original Hells Angels group merged with San Francisco's Market Street Commandos, and created the Hells Angels' second chapter. This chapter designed the "winged death" logo, which is essentially a skull with wings.

1954: The movie *The Wild One,* starring Marlon Brando, is released. The Hollywood movie was inspired by the rumble at Hollister.

1960s: During the 1960s, several new HAMC chapters emerged along the California coastline. Once Sonny Barger founded the Oakland chapter, the group was truly organized. Barger emerged as a leader for the HAMC movement. Under Barger's leadership, the chapters incorporated, wrote by-laws and codes of conduct, and created tattoos, patches, and clubhouses. During this time, the Hells Angels were accused of rape in a high-profile case in Monterey. Potentially, the legal fees for this case were incentive for the Hells Angels to start trafficking in amphetamines. Ultimately, the rape suspects were acquitted, but this case was followed by repeated arrests and acquittals, begging the question: overzealous arrests or covert deals? Over the course of both the 1960s and '70s, the FBI catalogued a voluminous report on the group, now available through the Freedom of Information Act.

1967: Hunter S. Thompson's *Hell's Angels: A Strange and Terrible Saga* was published. Initially, *The Nation* sent Thompson out in the mid-1960s to write an article about the Hells Angels. He ultimately ended up riding with them for over a year while researching his book, crystallizing his own self-named brand of gonzo journalism as he did his unconventional fieldwork.

1967: In *Electric Kool-Aid Acid Test*, published in 1967, Tom Wolfe writes of the relationship between the Hells Angels and the Grateful Dead. These groups maintained a surprising level of mutual respect, perhaps based on their shared objective to live their lives out on the road.

1967: Sonny Barger starred next to Jack Nicholson in the movie *Hells Angels on Wheels*.

1969: Sonny Barger also starred in *Hell's Angels '69*, a fictional account of the Hells Angels.

1969: The Hells Angels were hired to run security for the Rolling Stones concert at the Altamont Speedway, just outside of San Francisco, for 300,000 fans. During the song "Under My Thumb" (though people mistakenly remember it as "Sympathy for the Devil"), an eighteen-year-old fan rushed the stage and shot a Hells Angel in the arm, at which point the fan was repeatedly stabbed and stamped to death. This event became the basis for the 1970 documentary *Gimme Shelter*.

1969: The movie *Easy Rider* was released, continuing the cinematic love affair between film and the romance of the motorcycle on the open road.

1983: The Hells Angels release their own documentary titled *Hells Angels Forever*, with a sound track including music by Jerry Garcia and Willie Nelson.

1984: George Christie, president of the Ventura chapter of the HAMC, carried the Olympic torch for one mile.

1998: The Hells Angels celebrated their fiftieth anniversary

1999: The History Channel aired a documentary titled *In Search of History: Hells Angels.*

2001: Sonny Barger published his best-selling autobiography, titled *Hell's Angel: The Life and Times of Sonny Barger and the Hell's Angels Motorcycle Club*.

2003: Seven hundred police officers served eighty search warrants and arrested fifty-seven people in a raid of Hells Angels facilities. The arrests were a result of a two-year undercover investigation.

2004: In Canada, two Hells Angels members were sentenced for conspiring to murder and attempting to import 4,000 kg of cocaine from Colombia to Canada.

Other miscellaneous facts:

*On the average, HAMC members ride 20,000 miles a year.

*The term "81" is a metonym for the Hells Angels, "8" standing for "H," the eighth letter in the alphabet, and "1" standing for "A," the first letter in the alphabet.

SEVEN HEAVENLY PLACES THAT ARE UTTER HELL

1. HEAVEN'S GATE: This pleasant-sounding "place" is actually a cult that rose to infamy when the group arranged its own mass suicide in 1997, in the city of San Diego. Based on the promise of the Halle-Bopp comet's arrival, the cult members anticipated the comet's companion spaceship that would carry the cult members to a higher existence. This group was first written about in *Time* magazine in 1975. Organized by their leader, a former music professor at a Texas college, Marshall Herff Applewhite, Heaven's Gate members made their living as Web page designers, though their former occupations ranged from a beauty queen to an actress on *Star Trek*. Originally, Applewhite led the group with his companion, Bonnie Lu Nettles. The couple first changed their names to "Bo" and "Peep" but then changed them again to "Ti" and "Do," respectively. In 1997, thirty-nine members

consumed a mixture of pudding or applesauce mixed with vodka and phenobarbital, and ensured their death with plastic bags for suffocation. Authorities who discovered the bodies reported that six of the eighteen men who killed themselves had been surgically castrated some time well before the suicide. The suicide's timing was specifically prompted by the arrival of the Halle-Bopp comet. Beside each body was a travel bag, though the contents of the bags were not reported.

2. THE CROSSROADS: Everyone knows the myth of two crossed roads or has seen the movie (1986). According to legend, bluesman Robert Johnson made a pact with the devil at the intersection of two roads. In exchange for his soul, Johnson asked that Satan give him talent. Most would agree that Satan kept his side of the bargain; Johnson is considered the godfather of Delta blues. On the other hand, according to legend, Johnson was the victim of an untimely death, purportedly by poison, and those who have performed the song ("Crossroad Blues") over the years, such as Eric Clapton, Lynyrd Skynyrd, and the Allman Brothers, have also experienced tragedy. Many believe the song itself is a curse. So while the crossroads may seem fertile ground for your inner opportunist, consider the cost.

3. MUHAMMADAN 7TH HEAVEN: *see page 49.*

4. HEAVEN'S PLAYGROUND: Billed as "a special waiting area for pets," this quasi-recreational spot is a place you dare not go unless you are, essentially, a dead dog, or other breed of "former pet." The "playground" exists only in cyberspace, but offers various options for grieving pet owners, including a place to contribute pet poems and pet memorials, with a special place for pets that died in the wake of 9/11. Against a cyber-starry night scene, visitors to this virtual cemetery will be treated with a muzak version of "That's What Friends Are For."

5. 7TH HEAVEN: While the idea of a wholesome television show with Christian values may be an easy sell to some, this show, which first aired in 1996, has some of the most annoying characters (or actors) ever known to network television. Whatever the origin or concept may be, the results are far from heavenly. The family is basically the

embodiment of Pollyannaism, at various ages. The twins have a bizarre tendency to speak or move in unison, which is more creepy than cuddly. Ostensibly, everyone on this show dyes his or her hair though the suggestion is that they're genetically angelic (as in "blonde").

6. MERMAID'S PURSE: Though seductive by name, this aquatic "purse" is actually an egg sac laid by a female angel shark. Though these sharks are hardly interested in humans, they will bite to defend themselves as well as their young.

7. SOUTH OF HEAVEN: Though this might sound like a mere detour from the pearly gates, *South of Heaven* is actually a 1988 album released by the thrash/speed metal band Slayer. With the exception of speed metal fans, this album might constitute a personal hell for most listeners who anticipate something melodic. No sweet sound of harps here.

THE SEVEN HEAVENLY VIRTUES

1. Faith
2. Hope
3. Charity
4. Fortitude
5. Justice
6. Temperance
7. Prudence

See the Seven Deadly Sins, page 89

THE CONTRARY VIRTUES

(Defined in "Battle for the Soul," an epic poem written by Prudentius in the fifth century. Living by these virtues might be considered an "antidote" to the Seven Deadly Sins.)

1. Humility
2. Kindness
3. Abstinence
4. Chastity
5. Patience
6. Liberality
7. Diligence

THE SEVEN CORPORAL WORKS OF MERCY

From Medieval Catechisms

1. Feed the hungry
2. Give drink to the thirsty
3. Give shelter to strangers
4. Clothe the naked
5. Visit the sick
6. Minister to prisoners
7. Bury the dead

GUARDIAN ANGELS, A BRIEF HISTORY

Founded by Curtis Sliwa, a former manager at a McDonald's in a crime-infested section of the Bronx, the Guardian Angels are a group of volunteers who patrol city streets and subways as watchdogs, occasionally making citizen's arrests. Marked by their red berets, this group formed their first patrol in 1979. Sliwa was already famous locally for his cleanup efforts in the South Bronx by the time he led the now-famous Angels. The first patrol he formed was called the Magnificent Thirteen, and they rode the most dangerous subways, without weapons, to defend passengers from muggers who had become increasingly active on certain train lines. The group later changed its name to the Guardian Angels to counter the impression and character of the Hells Angels, who had formed in 1948. Currently, the Guardian Angels have chapters all over the country, including those in Florida, Nevada, Illinois, and Georgia, along with international chapters in Asia, Europe, and South America. In the United States, the Guardian Angels now focus on self-defense as well as their more recent CyberAngels program, which patrols the Internet for unsavory Web sites that put young people at risk.

Traditionally, guardian angels are angels assigned to specific souls, and some people believe that every soul has his or her own guardian angel. St. Jerome says, "How great the dignity of the soul, since each one has from his birth an angel commissioned to guard it."
See Feast of Guardian Angels, page 58, and Hells Angels, page 20

ANGEL WATER

(an old Spanish cosmetic, popularly used as perfume)

Mix:

Angelica	Rose
Myrtle	Orange
Flower waters	Ambergris

Or (the original recipe):

Rose	Trefoil
Lavender	Angelica

OTHER ANGELIC COSMETICS

1. Dream Angels Heavenly by Victoria Secret
2. Dream Angels Divine by Victoria Secret
3. Dream Angels Halo by Victoria Secret
4. Estée Lauder Lucidity Compact Angel Edition
5. Angel by Thierry Muggler (deodorant, mask, shower mousse, for both men and women, with scents ranging from "oriental and woody" to "oriental-fruity")
6. Angel Schlesser Femme
7. Angel Schlesser Homme
8. Clinique Different Lipstick in Angel Red ("moisture-enriched, long lasting . . .")
9. Clinique Chubby Stick in Angel Kiss ("liner and lipstick in one")
10. Clinique Eyeshadow Duo in Angel Eyes Smooth ("velvety pair of complementary color eyeshadows.")

BUDDHIST HOT HELLS

Note: The uppermost hell, number 1, begins 1,000 leagues below the surface of the earth. Several thousand leagues separate each hell from one another. Each hell contains subhells, usually sixteen, through which the sinner passes. In Buddhism, hell is temporary and, once the sinner's karmic energy is used up, one leaves hell and is reborn in another state.

Sanskrit	English	Punishment	Karma
1. Samjiva	Hell of Constant Reviving	Living as the one killed; those who hunted animals are eaten from the inside out by maggots. The tormented one is continuously revived and killed again.	The Body
2. Kala Sutra	Black Lines (or Rope) Hell	Reborn as a result of stealing; the tormented's body is nailed down and tied up with rope soaked in black ink. The bodies are cut up with burning saws. Note: there are subhells in this hell, where the tormented drinks molten copper and is stabbed with spears or blinded by a large, eyeball-plucking bird.	
3. Samghata	Squeezing Hell	Those tormented are here for "sexual misbehavior" and are tempted with beautiful sexual objects, then squeezed, crushed, cut up, sliced open, and burned up, while never reaching the sexual object/beloved.	
4. Raurava	Screaming Hell	Substance abusers are tortured here when demons pry their mouths open and pour boiling liquids down their throats, burning their bodies from the inside out.	

5. Maha Raurava	Great Screaming Hell	Liars are sent here, where snakes gnaw inside their bodies and pull out their tongues, burning their mouths.	The Mouth
6. Tapana	Burning Hell	Here, heretics burn up. Other hells are "cool as snowflakes compared to this hell."	The Thinking Mind
7. Pratapana	Great Burning Hell	For those who have sexually defiled religion (raping a monk or nun). This hell is ten times hotter then number 6. The tormented are dragged over the universe with iron hooks and tied to a spiked floor, where demons shove sharp-toothed worms up the tormented's buttocks. The worms eat the insides and crack open the tormented's head to escape.	
8. Avici	Hell without Cease	This hell is reserved for the gravest sinners, who have committed one of the Five Great Premeditated Sins: killing one's father, killing one's mother, harming the Buddha, disrupting the sangha, or killing an arhat. This hell is considered so far below the earth that a sinner here falls 2,000 years before even reaching it. The residents here are envious of the other hells.	

BUDDHIST COLD HELLS
The Eight "Cold" Hells Located at the Edge of the Buddhist Universe, According to Northern Buddhism*

1. ARBUDA: "chapped"—In this hell, even Susie Chapstick couldn't help you. Those caught here are submerged, naked, into ice water until they're covered in ice blisters. Anyone who's touched the ice-cream man's "dry ice" knows how these hurt.
2. NIRARBUDA: "deeply chapped"—In this hell, those ice blisters (see Arbuda) become open sores.
3. ATATA: Inhabitants are too cold to speak or cry.
4. HAHAVA: In this hell, one's tongue is paralyzed and it's difficult to breathe.
5. AHAHA: In this hell, one's jaws and teeth are clenched (this hell sounds alarmingly similar to what many of us experience each day).
6. UTPALA: "flower"—In this hell, the victim's open sores (see Nirarbuda) turn blue, the color of utpala flowers.
7. PADMA: "lotus hell."
8. PUNDARIKA: "petal"—In this deceitfully sweet-sounding hell, the victim's flesh falls away from the bones like petals falling off a flower. If that isn't enough to keep you on the straight and narrow, be warned that this fate continues with an orgy of iron-beaked birds plus some insects feasting on the falling flesh.

*Unlike the concept of Hell in the Christian religion, "hell" in Buddhism is not an eternal state. Instead, it's a temporary place where a sinner endures punishment before reincarnation.

HA-HA FOR HELLIONS, A JOKE
Sue over the property

Did you know that heaven and hell are actually right next to each other? They are separated by a big chain-link fence. Well, one day hell was having a big party and it got a little out of hand. God heard the ruckus and arrived to find his fence completely smashed by the wild partyers.

He called the devil over and said, "Look, Satan, you have to rebuild this fence." Satan agreed. The next day God noticed that the devil had completely rebuilt the fence, but it was two feet farther into heaven than before.

"Satan!" beckoned God. "You have to take that fence down and put it back where it belongs!"

"Yeah? What if I don't?" replied the devil.

"I'll sue you if I have to," answered God.

"Sure," laughed Satan. "Where are you going to find a lawyer?"

TERMS FOR HEAVEN IN THE BIBLE

1. Paradise (Luke 23:43; 2 Cor. 12:3; Rev. 2:7)
2. the new heaven, the new Jerusalem (Rev. 21:1–2)
3. the holy city of Jerusalem (Rev. 21:10)
4. the king of glory (Ps. 24:7), Crown of Glory (I Pet. 5:4)
5. the place of Abraham, in the parable of the rich man and Lazarus (Luke 16:19–31)
6. the kingdom of heaven (Matt. 5:3)
7. great reward (Matt. 5:12)
8. life (Matt. 7:14)
9. life everlasting (Matt. 9:16)
10. the kingdom of the Father (Matt. 13:43)
11. the joy of the Lord (Matt. 25:21)
12. eternal life (Matt. 25:46)
13. the kingdom (Matt. 25:34)
14. the kingdom of God (Mark 9:46)
15. the kingdom of Christ (Luke 22:30)
16. the house of the Father (John 14:2)
17. incorrupt crown (I Cor. 9:25)
18. inheritance of Christ (Eph. 1:18)
19. crown of justice (2 Tim. 4:8)
20. crown of life (James 1:12)
21. the holy place (Heb. 9:12)
22. eternal inheritance (Heb. 9:15)

23. Mount Zion, the city of the living God, the heavenly Jerusalem (Heb. 12:22)
24. the new heaven, the new Jerusalem (Rev. 21:1–2)
25. the City (Rev. 22:2–3)

DESCRIPTIONS OF HEAVEN IN THE BIBLE

1. A sprawling city made of gold and glass. (Rev. 21:2, 15–17)
2. With thick walls—made of jasper, sapphire, chalcedony, emerald, sardonyx, carnelian, chrysolite, beryl, topaz, chrysoprase, jacinth, and amethyst—surrounding the city. (Rev. 21:17–20)
3. Twelve gates, each gate made of one single, enormous pearl. (Rev. 21:12–14, 21)
4. Naturally lit by God, Heaven requires neither the sun nor the moon for illumination. ("…and the Lamb is its lamp," Rev. 21:23–27)

SIX DESTINIES FOR REINCARNATION
According to Buddhism

1. The gods
2. Humans
3. Demons (asura)
4. Animals
5. Hungry ghosts (pretas)
6. Hell (nakara)

Note: at various points in Buddhist history, only five destinies were recognized; the third (demons) was left out. Generally, destines 1 through 3 were considered good, whereas 4 through 6 were considered bad.

SUGATI: good destiny, including reincarnation into a god, a human, or a demon.

DURGATI: a bad destiny, including reincarnation into an animal, a ghost, or return to hell.

WHEELS OF LIFE

In the Buddhist tradition, a wheel represents life in eternal rotation, also called samsara. The wheel is depicted in the clutches of the "Evil One," or Mara, the Buddhist devil. Across several national traditions (Tibetan, Indian, and Japanese), the wheel remains essentially the same. In the center are three causes of selfhood—hatred, spite, and sloth—along with six sections making up a middle ring of the wheel, which depict the six destinies for reincarnation (*see page 32*). Typically, though not always, an outermost ring is divided into twelve sections, and these sections represent the twelve karmic formations.

Japanese Wheel of Life

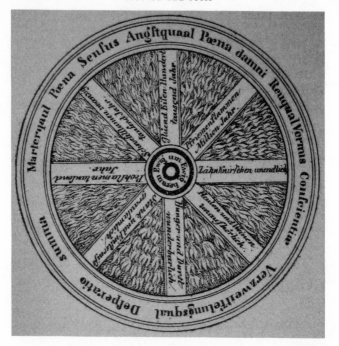

Schottel's Wheel of Life

Designed by Justus Georg Schottel, member of the Consistory of
Brunswick-Lüneberg and councillor to the duke. The wheel represents
the "iron wheel of eternal hell torture." He wrote:

> How much time and suffering, how much anxiety and
> torture of despair, must be gone through in hell, must be
> endured, borne, experienced and realized by hundreds, by
> thousands, by hundreds of thousands, by millions of years
> in burning pitch, in flaming sulphur, in red-hot iron, in
> poignant blow-pipe flames, with weeping and wailing and
> gnashing of teeth infinite; with hunger and thirst
> miraculous; in stench and darkness cruelly; before this
> wheel be turned around only once.

COCKTAIL BREAK:
ANGEL'S DELIGHT SHOOTER, A SAINTLY SWIG

0.5 oz Cointreau/triple sec
0.5 oz Plymouth gin
1 shot Single cream
Shake ingredients with ice and strain into a shot glass

MORE MATH: MYSTERY OF NUMBERS

Pythagoras held numbers to be the principle of all things; and perhaps they are when frequently added together with 8 prefixed. The two great principles of the sage were monad and duad, in other words, unity and quality. A modern philosopher has come out in the *Ontario Messenger* in favor of the number 3. He has roamed about in the storehouse of his memory and pulled down from the shelves everything young and old, good, bad, and indifferent, that bears a trinal character or aspects.

Three was the number of the Graces, the Fates, the Furies, the Syrens, the Gorgons and the Graeae—those infernal hags, who had but one eye and one tooth among them, which they used to borrow by turns, as they were to see company or to chew their cud.

Geryon had three bodies; Cerberus heads enough for them all, and Solomon has many opinions. There were three Triumvirates: Caesar, Pompey and Crassus; Augustus, Anthony and Lepsidus; and Andrews, Beville and Carewe.—This last is formed by one Trigliph too.

Apollo has his Tripod, and Neptune his Trident. One, two, three and away, was the word for starting at the Olympic races. And the ancients used to call thrice upon every corpse, to know if it could start any objections to its being interred. Which naturally leads me to Hades or Ades, the old fashion of distribution according to our good or bad deeds. It consisted of three provinces, Erebus, Tartarus and Elysium. Heaven, Hell and Purgatory—it had its three judges too; Minos, Alacus and Rhadamanthus. Its three rivers too, Plegethon, Cocytus and Acheron, with many other Triads too numerous and inconsiderable to mention.

—from *Freedom's Journal* (New York), March 14, 1829

To this he might have added that the three wise men of Gotham went to sea in a bowl; that a sentry says "who comes there?" three times, before he sends a bullet after a man; that a note of hand has three days' grace; and that a paper of tobacco costs three cents.

SUPERSTITIONS RELATED TO HEAVEN

1. When a shooting star appears, it's a baby's soul coming down from heaven.
2. A shooting star foretells the "death of Kings" (Shakespeare, *Richard the Second*).
3. If you put a stillborn baby in an open grave, the grave is an "open passport" to heaven for the next person buried there.
4. If you point at the moon nine times, you won't go to heaven.
5. Touching wood is a way of saying "Heaven, preserve us."
6. If you eat wedding cake at someone else's wedding, you will meet your mate, as destined in heaven.
7. If a lull occurs in conversation (especially at twenty before or twenty after the hour), it's an angel passing over.
8. If a cock crows at midnight, death is passing over the house.
9. When someone dies, open the windows so the Angel of Death can exit.

SUPERSTITIONS RELATED TO HELL

1. Burn your baby teeth as they fall out, or else you'll be looking for them later in a pail of blood, in hell.
2. The northern side of a graveyard designates hell.
3. Parsley supposedly grows only in the hands of the wicked. It goes "to hell and back" before it sprouts.
4. Black is the color of the devil, or Satan.
5. If you've misplaced something in your house, stick a pin in your chair and shout "I've pinned the devil" and the object will be found.
6. Outline your house or steps with a chalk design to keep the devil out.
7. If you speak of the devil, the devil will come.
8. The herb Saint-John's-wort supposedly protects people from the devil.

FESTIVALS OF THE DEAD

1. OBON: A Buddhist Festival of the Dead in July, according to the Western calendar, or in August, according the Chinese (lunar) calendar. During this festival, families hang paper lanterns in cemeteries where their family members are buried. These lanterns are decorated with a family's crest to guide the dead family members' spirits back to the family tomb or gravesite.

2. ALL SOULS' DAY: A Catholic holiday (November 2) that follows All Saints' Day. On this day, the living remember and honor those who have passed, while praying for their souls to travel from purgatory to heaven. Various traditions are observed on this day, including the creation of an altar upon which food for the dead is offered.

3. EL DIA DE LOS MUERTOS, OR DAY OF THE DEAD: This holiday is celebrated on November 2 each year in Mexico. During this holiday, those celebrating are honoring the return of the dead to earth. Families often spend the day in the cemetery visiting the graves of dead relatives, while eating candy, hot chocolate, and bread of the dead, or *pan de muerto*.

From Ryder-Waite tarot deck

BIBLE FIGURES WHO ASCENDED TO HEAVEN

1. Enoch (Gen. 5:24)
2. Elijah (2 Kings 2:1–12)
3. Jesus (Luke 24:51; Acts 1:9)
4. Paul (2 Cor. 12:2–4)
5. John (Rev. 4:1)

BEATIFIC BUMPER STICKERS

1. "Caution: Never Drive Faster Than Your Angels Can Fly"
2. "Angels: Don't Leave Home Without Them"
3. "Protected by Angels"
4. "People Plan . . . God Laughs . . . Just Wing It"
5. "Angel at Heart"
6. "Angels at Work: Prepare for Random Miracles"
7. "I Believe in Angels"
8. "Peace Is Possible: Allow the Angels to Inspire You"
9. "Angels Believe in Me"
10. "Angels Have PMS, Too"
11. "Heaven Is Just Out of This World"
12. "Heaven Is Real—Do You Have a Reservation?"

EXORCISMS

From *Rosemary's Baby* to *Poltergeist,* the film industry has made a mint off of exorcisms, while exposing millions of people to the ideas behind demon-ridding, in the broadest sense. Rumors circulated several years ago that the pope, himself, performed three exorcisms during his post. Though the Catholic Church has a long history of casting out demons from human bodies gone evil, or astray, the idea of exorcism exists in other religions as well, such as Shinto and some Native American religions.

Heaven and Hell

Movies with Exorcisms:

Rosemary's Baby (1968) • *Ghostbusters* (1984)
The Exorcist (1973, 2004) • *Naked Evil* (1966) • *Poltergeist* (1982)
Amityville Horror (1979)

Jesus casting out devils (after Schnorr von Carolsfeld)

Hosting Your Own Exorcism, A Guide

On January 26, 1999, the Vatican formally released a document approved by Pope John Paul II, which laid out the basics of the exorcism rite in Latin (*De Exorcismis*).

> Warning: Please look for signs of demon possession before performing this rite. Signs include speaking in tongues, Hulk-like strength, and unusual knowledge of distant entities (in time and/or space).

Step 1:Bishop Is Boss. Find a local bishop. An exorcism can occur only under the guidance of the local bishop.

Step 2: Procure Permission from Demon-hoarder. The diabolically possessed must consent to the rite.

Step 3: Renew Your Subscription. Though the *Roman Book of Rites* contains classic instructions for the rite, this text was recently revised in a ten-year editing process. The revised instructions include both steps and prayers.

Step 4: Get Thee to the Church on Time. With the exception of an ailing demon-hoarder, the possessed should be led to a church, and away from a crowd (the people will always be drawn to a good exorcism!).

Step 5: Push the Cross. Plaster the head and breast of said victim with a crucifix or a relic of the saints.

Step 6: Priestly Projection. The leader of this rite must speak in an authoritative tone, with confidence but also with humility. Holy water should be on hand for unexpected swelling or disfiguration of the afflicted.

Step 7: Lady Friends. If the afflicted is a woman, several women "of good repute" should be available for the rite, to hold on to the afflicted.

Step 8: Read the Holy Writ. Do not improvise. Use the words offered in the text.

Step 9: The Riot Act. Warn the newly demon-free subject to resist all temptation to sin, lest the evil spirit returns.

CONTACTING ANGELS, SOME SUGGESTIONS

1. CHANNELING: Various new age counselors offer sessions in which the counselor will "listen" to the client's personal angel and report back.
2. PRAYER: Self-explanatory.
3. MEDITATION/VISUALIZATION: Through meditation and visualization, you can become more sensitive to the presence of angels.
4. CRYSTALS: This is a not-so-easy process of asking a cherub to "charge" your crystal. If cherubim were willing to do this, wouldn't they also speak as well?

5. WRITING LETTERS: This might be the greatest stretch for the rational thinkers among you. Don't forget to date and sign the letter. You can "mail" it by placing it under your pillow, or burning it. Be creative.

6. WEARING THE RIGHT COLORS: This may be the least-known approach. Purportedly, various angels are partial to specific colors. Serpahim angels like red, cherubim like blue, and Michael likes several colors: deep green, blue, gold, and rose. Gabriel is more of an autumn angel, preferring neutral shades of brown (tan) along with dark greens.

CELESTIAL COUTURE

PRIZE FOR THE BEST ANGEL GETUP: This prize goes (hands down) to Metatron, formerly known as Enoch in his pre-ascension days. According to Jewish tradition, Metatron is second only to God in rank. With a gargantuan stature, Metatron sports thirty-six pairs of wings, more eyes than can be counted, and a face made of lightness itself. Though this trendsetting, go-his-own-way kind of angel has at least a hundred different names in various writings, there is only one Metatron.
See Ten Heavens and their Rulers, page 43

SECOND PRIZE FOR ANGEL GETUP: The mysterious Tall Angel takes this award. Moses encounters this unnamed figure in the third heaven, and describes the angel as possessing 70,000 heads. To be safe, we should accept this as an estimate, at best.

THIRD PRIZE FOR ANGEL GETUP: According to the Koran, the archangel Michael is covered with saffron hairs, each hair with a million faces, each face with a million eyes. Each eye sheds 700,000 tears and each tear becomes a cherub.

GETTING TO HEAVEN

1. UNIVERSALISM: Everyone will go to heaven.
2. CALVINISM: Those who will go to heaven were predestined by God to go there; it has nothing to do with deeds in life.
3. BUDDHISM: Those with good karma will be reborn in a heaven (Buddhism holds that several heavens exist).

4. ISLAM: Muslims will inherit heaven or, alternatively, pass through hell temporarily and ultimately reside in heaven if there is "one atom of faith in their hearts." Those who do not believe at all in the faith will go to hell for eternal damnation.

5. JUDAISM: Various forms of Judaism (Conservative, Orthodox, Reform, Humanist) differ in their belief in the afterlife. Most variations still hold that the soul makes various stops (the angel of silence, the angel of death, purgatory, among others) along the way to Gan Eden, or heaven.

See Gan Eden, page 2, and angel of silence, page 48
See Ticket to Heaven, page 54

From Heradis von Lansperg's *Hortus Deliciarum*.
The *Hortus Deliciarum* was written in the late twelfth century for monks, and this illustration warned them of various temptations, including money, laziness, even gardening.

EIGHT SIGNIFICANT ANGELS AND THE MEANING OF THEIR NAMES

1. Lucifer .... Light Bearer
2. Raphael .... Healing of El
3. Camael .... He Who Sees El
4. Raguel .... Ally of El
5. Gabriel .... Strong One of El
6. Sarakiel .... Prince of El
7. Phaniel .... Face of El
8. Michael .... Who Is Like El

Note: "El" is short for the Hebrew word *Elohim*, which translates into "Lord," in English, but is "higher" than the other word for Lord, Adonai.

TEN HEAVENS AND THEIR RULERS

(from the Book of Enoch)

Enoch, a seventh-generation descendant of Adam, was ultimately transformed into the angel Metatron, once in heaven. The Book of Enoch is composed of multiple writings concerning Enoch's travels and visions, authored between the second century BCE and the sixth century CE. Though little attention was paid to them for many centuries, scholars have mined them more recently and many churches have recognized the texts as an important part of the liturgical canon.

Heaven	Ruler	Description
First Heaven	Gabriel	Filled with angels controlling the weather—the rain, the snow—as well as astronomer angels, and the winds and clouds themselves. This heaven is closer to earth than the other nine heavens.
Second Heaven	Raphael	Filled with fallen angels, a dark region of punishment.

Third Heaven	Anahel	This is a heaven filled with two opposing landscapes—one hell-like and the other paradisiacal. Also: here lies the motherlode of manna, or angel bread. *See angel bread recipe, page 56*
Fourth Heaven	Michael	Remember the song "Michael, Row Your Boat Ashore," the milk and honey on the other side? The fourth heaven is filled with rivers made of milk, honey, and wine, along with exquisite music and singing, Holy Jerusalem, and a gold temple.
Fifth Heaven	Satan	Also a grim scene (see Second Heaven), this "heaven" is filled with prisoners called Watchers. Watchers, bizarrely enough, are angels who mingled and rendezvoused with human women.
Sixth Heaven		This is the place for the smarty-pants angels, those intellectual angels who study astronomy, along with human behavior and the physical world.
Seventh Heaven		A realm filled with light as well as several orders of angels.
Eighth Heaven		Here, the twelve signs of the zodiac reside, along with those angels responsible for changing the seasons.
Ninth Heaven		A realm containing the aforementioned zodiac signs' habitats.
Tenth Heaven		God.

NIKE ISN'T JUST A SHOE

Though "Nike" may bring sneakers to mind, Nike is the Greek winged goddess of victory, a precursor and extremely determinate influence on the now popular image of the winged angel associated with Christianity. Nike was a gal-pal of powerful Athena, the queen of heaven. Nike's likeness was most likely influenced by the image of Isis.

BON MOTS FOR BEELZEBUB

Between the Devil and the deep blue sea: trapped between two options that are equally treacherous.

Speak of the Devil: response to a person's appearance immediately after the person is mentioned.

Sup with the Devil: consort with an evil or untrustworthy person.

Better the Devil you know: it's better to deal with a person whose flaws you know than risk dealings with a person who may have other/worse deficiencies.

A Devil of a _____: a negative example of something.

To sell one's soul to the Devil: to do anything to succeed in one's mission.

Play Devil's advocate: argue the opposite view of the one truly believed by the arguer.

The world, the flesh, and the Devil: entire catalog of sins and temptations.

The Devil is in the details: refers to issues still unknown, which defy understanding or transparency.

Devil takes the hindmost: each man for himself. The Latin version reads: *Occupet extremum scabies*, or "May the itch take the one who is last."

The Devil looks after his own.

The Devil is not so black as he is painted.

Truth makes the Devil blush.

An idle brain is the Devil's workshop: a lazy brain is fodder for sin.

God sends meat, but the Devil sends cooks.

Heaven and Hell

Where God builds a church, the Devil builds a chapel: good and evil always coexist.

Why should the Devil have all the best tunes?

It is easier to raise the Devil than to lay him: sin is always an easier path than goodness and virtue.

Never bid the Devil good morrow until you meet him: never say you wouldn't do something until you meet temptation and reject it.

The Devil finds work for idle hands to do: people with free time are easy targets for sinful acts and thoughts.

He who sups with the Devil should have a long spoon.

The Devil makes his Christmas pies of lawyers' tongues and clerks' fingers.

Get a beggar on horseback, and he'll ride with the Devil.

Give a thing, and take a thing, to wear the Devil's gold ring: a rhyme used by schoolchildren when someone offers something and then requests it back.

The Devil to pay: most likely a reference to a Faustian exchange, though the phrase also may have nautical origins. The "devil" is a seam on a ship that is hard to reach and "pay" may refer to the caulking or tarring that the seam required. In 1738, Jonathan Swift wrote: "I must be with my Wife on Tuesday, or there will be the Devil and all to pay."

Handsome Devil: Good-looking guy.

The White Devil: tennis, seventeenth century.

Devil's dozen: thirteen total.

Hell hath no fury like a woman scorned.

England is the paradise of women, the hell of horses, and the purgatory of servants.

The road to hell is paved with good intentions.

Like a bat out of hell: as fast as possible, of a wild manner.

Not a cat in hell's chance: not possible at all.

From hell: terrible, obnoxious.

Be hell on: be difficult to.

Heaven and Hell

Raise hell: cause a ruckus.

Not a hope in hell.

Get the hell out of _____: leave a place quickly.

(Ride) hell for leather: as fast as possible, make tracks.

Until hell freezes over: eternity, or almost eternity.

There will be hell to pay: there will be trouble as a consequence.

Play (merry) hell with: disrupt or disturb.

Go to hell and back: endure an odious adventure or experience.

Give someone hell: unleash an attack on someone.

All hell broke loose: chaos ensued.

Hell's half acre: an extreme distance.

Come hell or high water: regardless of what obstacles are posed (a later version of Between the Devil and the deep blue sea).

See Proverbs from Paradise, page 124

BABY NAME FINDER, PART I

Alavi	Heavenly, Divine	Arabic	Male
Angela	Heavenly Messenger	Greek	Female
Aolani	Heavenly Cloud	Hawaiian	Female
Araceli	Altar of Heaven	Latin	Female
Celeste	Heavenly	Latin	Female
Devi	Resides in Heaven	Hindu	Female
Geoffrey	Heavenly Place	English	Male
Hera	Queen of Heaven	Greek	Female
Juno	Queen of Heaven	Latin	Female
Kalani	Heaven	Hawaiian	Male
Lani	Sky, Heaven	Hawaiian	Female
Leilani	Heavenly Child	Hawaiian	Female
Noelani	Beautiful Girl from Heaven	Hawaiian	Female
Okelani	From Heaven	Hawaiian	Female
Urania	Heavenly, Muse of Astronomy	Greek	Female

Arcelia	Treasure, Altar of Heaven	Spanish	Female
Borak	The Lightning	Arabic	Male
	(Al Borak was the horse that		
	brought Muhammad from		
	earth to the seventh heaven)		
Celesse	Heavenly	French	Female
Falak	Heaven	Hindu	Male
Gimle	New Heaven	Norse	Female
Jannat	Heaven, Garden	Arabic	Female
Meena	Starling, Heaven, Glass	Arabic	Female
Minau	Heaven	Persian	Female
Olympas	Heavenly	Biblical	Female
Ridhwan	Name of the keeper of the	Arabic	Male
	Gates of Heaven		
Sheiramoth	From Heaven	Hebrew	Female
Shemiramoth	The Height of Heavens	Biblical	Male
Talya	Dew of Heaven	Hebrew	Female
Urian	From Heaven	Greek	Male
Yggsdrasil	Tree that Binds Heaven,	Norse	Female
	Hell, and Earth		

See Baby Name Finder, Part II, page 92

AN ANGEL PROFILE: DUMAH

DUMAH: 1. The angel of silence and stillness of death ("Dumah" means silence in Aramaic). 2. The patron angel of Egypt (one of seventy patron angels protecting nations). 3. Guardian angel of the fourteenth gate.

4. Popular figure in Yiddish folklore (see Isaac B. Singer's work). 5. Considered by some to be the prince of hell. 6. According to Judaism, Dumah asks each Jewish person who dies his/her Jewish name.

SEVEN HEAVENS OF THE MUHAMMADANS*

1. SILVER: The "stars are hung out like lamps on golden chains."
2. GOLD: This heaven is the domain of John the Baptist and Jesus.
3. PEARL: Azrael is stationed here, writing down the names of newborns and crossing out the names of the dead.
4. WHITE GOLD: The angel of tears is here, crying for the sins of humankind.
5. SILVER: The Avenging Angel stays here, presiding over "elemental fire."
6. RUBY AND GARNET: Moses is here. The Guardian Angel of heaven and earth is also here. The landscape is half-snow, half-fire.
7. DIVINE LIGHT: The light is considered too beautiful to describe in words. Abraham rules this realm. Each inhabitant is bigger than the whole earth and has 70,000 heads; each head has 70,000 faces, each face has 70,000 mouths, each mouth has 70,000 tongues, and each tongue speaks 70,000 languages.

*Note: According to the Muslim faith, one's soul reaches one of these levels of heaven, according to the righteousness with which one led his/her life. *See Seven Hells of the Muhammadans, page 80*

SATANIC BUMPER STICKERS

1. "The Devil Is Pro-Choice—Read John 8:44"
2. "In the Sentence of Life the Devil May Be a Comma, but DO NOT LET Him Be the PERIOD!"
3. "God Is My Co-pilot, but the Devil Is my Bombardier"
4. "Never Give the Devil a Ride! He Will Always Want to Drive"
5. "Give Satan an Inch and He'll Be a Ruler"
6. "Satan Can't Bring you Down any Further than your Knees"

7. "Dyslexic Devil"
8. "There Ain't no Devil. It's Just God When He's Drunk"
9. "Taking Back What the Devil Stole from Us"
10. "Decaffeinated Coffee Is the Devil's Blend"
11. "I Was Born Horny"
12. "God Gave Man the Truth . . . and the Devil Helped Us Turn it into Religion"
13. "Sexy Devil"
14. "The Devil Made Me Do It!"
15. "The Devil Wants to Control You; God Wants to Lead You"
16. "The Road to Hell is Bumper to Bumper; Make a U-turn"
17. "Heaven Doesn't Want Me, and Hell Is Afraid I'll Take Over"

EXCERPT: "CAPTAIN STORMFIELD'S VISIT TO HEAVEN" BY MARK TWAIN

"By George, I've arrived at last—and at the wrong place, just as I expected!"

Then I fainted. I don't know how long I was insensible, but it must have been a good while, for, when I came to, the darkness was all gone and there was the loveliest sunshine and the balmiest, fragrantest air in its place. And there was such a marvellous world spread out before me—such a glowing, beautiful, bewitching country. The things I took for furnaces were gates, miles high, made all of flashing jewels, and they pierced a wall of solid gold that you couldn't see the top of, nor yet the end of, in either direction. I was pointed straight for one of these gates, and a-coming like a house afire. Now I noticed that the skies were black with millions of people, pointed for those gates. What a roar they made, rushing through the air! The ground was as thick as ants with people, too—billions of them, I judge.

I lit. I drifted up to a gate with a swarm of people, and when it was my turn the head clerk says, in a business-like way—"Well, quick! Where are you from?"

"San Francisco," says I.

"San Fran—WHAT?" says he.

50

"San Francisco."

He scratched his head and looked puzzled, then he says—"Is it a planet?"

By George, Peters, think of it! "PLANET?" says I; "it's a city. And moreover, it's one of the biggest and finest and—"

"There, there!" says he, "no time here for conversation. We don't deal in cities here. Where are you from in a GENERAL way?"

"Oh," I says, "I beg your pardon. Put me down for California."

I had him AGAIN, Peters! He puzzled a second, then he says, sharp and irritable—

"I don't know any such planet—is it a constellation?"

"Oh, my goodness!" says I. "Constellation, says you? No—it's a State."

"Man, we don't deal in States here. WILL you tell me where you are from IN GENERAL—AT LARGE, don't you understand?"

"Oh, now I get your idea," I says. "I'm from America,—the United States of America."

Peters, do you know I had him AGAIN? If I hadn't I'm a clam! His face was as blank as a target after a militia shooting-match. He turned to an under clerk and says—

"Where is America? WHAT is America?"

The under clerk answered up prompt and says—

"There ain't any such orb."

"ORB?" says I. "Why, what are you talking about, young man? It ain't an orb; it's a country; it's a continent. Columbus discovered it; I reckon likely you've heard of HIM, anyway. America—why, sir, America—"

"Silence!" says the head clerk. "Once for all, where—are—you— FROM?"

"Well," says I, "I don't know anything more to say—unless I lump things, and just say I'm from the world."

"Ah," says he, brightening up, "now that's something like! WHAT world?"

Peters, he had ME, that time. I looked at him, puzzled, he looked at me, worried. Then he burst out—

"Come, come, what world?"

Says I, "Why, THE world, of course."

"THE world!" he says. "H'm! there's billions of them! . . . Next!"

That meant for me to stand aside. I done so, and a sky-blue man with seven heads and only one leg hopped into my place. I took a walk. It just occurred to me, then, that all the myriads I had seen swarming to that gate, up to this time, were just like that creature. I tried to run across somebody I was acquainted with, but they were out of acquaintances of mine just then. So I thought the thing all over and finally sidled back there pretty meek and feeling rather stumped, as you may say.

"Well?" said the head clerk.

"Well, sir," I says, pretty humble, "I don't seem to make out which world it is I'm from. But you may know it from this—it's the one the Saviour saved."

He bent his head at the Name. Then he says, gently—

"The worlds He has saved are like to the gates of heaven in number—none can count them. What astronomical system is your world in?—perhaps that may assist..."

SOME COMPOUNDS WITH "HEAVEN"

heaven-given • heaven-guided • heaven-descended
heaven-kissing • heaven-exalted • heaven-bred
heaven-inspired • heaven-begot • heaven-aspiring
heaven-warring • heaven-taught

POESY PRIMER FOR PARADISE
Words to Keep Handy When Writing a
Rhyming Poem on Heaven

Leaven .... used to make bread rise
Seven .... number
Eleven .... number
Estefan (Devon, Evan) .... proper noun, names
Previn .... surname of famed musician André

Preven .... emergency contraception (the "morning after pill")

Genevan .... of Geneva

Break even .... to neither gain nor lose

A DEMON PROFILE: MARA

According to Buddhism, Mara is the personifcation of evil. Also called the *Papiyan*, which means "very wicked," Mara represents pleasures of the ego, along with sensuality, sin, and death; he is the enemy of Buddha and, consequently, the obstacle to Buddhahood.

PEOPLE/BEINGS YOU MIGHT FIND IN HEAVEN

1. Angels
2. God (as Father, Son, and Holy Ghost)
3. Allah
4. Brahma, or *pitamaha*
5. Vishnu

A DIVINE DICTIONARY OF ANGELIC APPELLATION

Heaven 17: Made up of three men, this 1980s band created some of the most popular synth-funk-pop ever made. The band's name was taken from a record sleeve featured in *Clockwork Orange*. The band's influences included Roxy Music, David Bowie, and Parliament, along with heavy synth mavens such as Kraftwerk. The three Heaven 17 band members started out as part of Human League but then broke off from HL. Ultimately, the two bands competed against each other on the charts.

HEAVEN (London): A gay nightclub in London.

HEAVEN: Healthier Environment through the Abatement of Vehicle Emissions and Noise. This project ran from 2000 to 2003 in several major European cities.

TICKET TO HEAVEN™: This organization offers a symbolic ticket to heaven, as a material commitment to live a "good and pure life." Available for all religions. With your purchase, you receive one ticket with your name and international registration number, one Certificate of Authenticity, and a wallet-sized testimonial card. Tickets currently cost $15.00, plus shipping costs ($4.95 domestic, $9.95 international—they must be heavy!).

TREE OF HEAVEN: A Chinese tree, similar to a sumac. It prefers shade.

HOG HEAVEN: An extremely pleasing situation.

GATE OF HEAVEN CEMETERY: Cemetery located in Hawthorne, New York. Babe Ruth is buried here.

THE TEMPLE OF HEAVEN: Located south of Beijing, the Temple of Heaven was built in 1420. Architecturally unique, the magnificent temple and its surrounding buildings cover five times the area of the Forbidden City. Over 700 years ago, emperors prayed in the temple for good harvests. The layout of the temple considers complex religious and cultural cosmography. The twenty-eight columns inside the Hall of Prayer are divided—four for the seasons of the year, twelve for the months of the year, and twelve outer columns, each to represent a two-hour increment of a day. Though common people were not allowed into the Temple of Heaven in its day, thousands of visitors now come to the temple each day. Early in the morning, visitors will see groups of people around the temple, practicing tai chi, karate, and sword fighting. In 1998 the Temple of Heaven was added to the World Cultural Heritage List.

MANDATE OF HEAVEN: A Chinese concept first introduced by the Zhou dynasty, created to generate a sense of authority concerning a king or emperor's right to rule, governance that (they claimed) was ordained and blessed by heaven. "Mandate of heaven" was also the era name of the Qing empire in China. Each empire in China was given a name for the period of years over which it reigned.

OUR FATHER, WHO ART IN HEAVEN: The first line of "The Lord's Prayer," or *Pater Noster*. Jesus Christ gave this prayer to the apostles when they asked him how to pray. Various versions exist, including the Roman Catholic version, which differs slightly.

ANGELS ON HORSEBACK: A British appetizer consisting of oysters wrapped in bacon, served on toast.

Recipe for Angels on Horseback

Servings: 25 appetizers
Ingredients:
1 pint fresh oysters
Bacon slices, cut in thirds
¼ cup chopped fresh parsley
½ tsp. garlic salt
Wooden toothpicks

Drain oysters. Place an oyster on each piece of bacon. Sprinkle with parsley and garlic salt. Wrap bacon around oyster and secure with wooden toothpick. Place angels on broiler rack, approximately 4 inches from heat source, and broil 3 to 4 minutes. Turn carefully and broil on other side if desired. Cook only until bacon is done, being careful not to overcook oysters. Serve with mixture of mayonnaise, mustard, and horseradish.

Chef Kathleen Morrison, www.foodgeeks.com.

See Cookbook, page 114

ANGELICA: A fragrant herb related to parsley whose stalks are sometimes used for cake decorations. The herb's name came from its use to counteract poison and disease. Also, this herb was used in an early Spanish cosmetic.

ANGELICAL STONE: A stone carried by Dr. John Dee, an astrologer employed by Queen Elizabeth I. Dee claimed this stone was given to him by the angels Raphael and Gabriel, and he used it to practice a form of divination called scrying. Today, the stone is in the British Museum.

Heaven and Hell

ANGEL BREAD: Also known as "manna," angel bread, a honey cake–like treat, is a source of both physical and spiritual sustenance, which appears from heaven throughout the Bible. In the Book of Exodus, the Israelites receive heaven-sent manna. Amazingly, the manna served as the Israelites plat du jour for over forty years, while they traveled through the wilderness. For a fat-free version for mere mortals, those who cannot wait for divine intervention, please see below.

Date Manna Bread

2 cups organic wheat, sprouted
½ lb dates (or more)
1 cup raisins
¼ teaspoon cloves
¼ teaspoon cinnamon

Place the sprouted wheat in a food processor and process until it is ground up and pasty. Add flour until it is doughy. Add dates, raisins, and spices and process a little more to mix. Form into small loaves or one larger loaf. Bake in a slow oven (300°F) for about 2.5 hours. Use your imagination and change this to suit your own tastes.

—courtesy of Barb Beck of Alberta, Canada

ANGEL WINGS: A lovely species of clam found mostly in the Caribbean.

ANGEL'S TRUMPET: A small tree native to South America, whose blossoms are large trumpet-shaped flowers.

ANGEL DUST: A hallucinogenic drug, also called: a peace pill; zoot; hog; tic; rocket fuel; and crystal. This illegal drug is swallowed as a liquid, pill, or capsule, smoked inside a cigarette or joint (crystal supergrass), or injected. The drug was invented in the 1950s as an anesthetic but discontinued in 1965 due to undesirable side effects, including delusional and irrational thinking, plus irritability. If you grew up watching a lot of "Say No to Drugs" movies/promos, this drug is the one that made the boy/girl jump out the window, thinking s/he could fly. Symptoms including tics, garbled speech, and depression can last up to a year after taking angel dust.

Heaven and Hell

ANGEL BED: A bed that has no posts.

ANGEL GOLD: Gold.

ANGEL SHOT: A kind of chain shot used in naval warfare. A chain shot is a device comprised of two cannon balls attached by chain.

ANGEL SHARK: These bottom dwellers grow up to seven feet in length and are named after their unusual winglike fins. They eat a healthy diet replete with fish, crustaceans, and mollusks.

ANGEL HAIR: (*noun*) 1. Lace-weight wool 2. Thin, long strands of pasta, also called capellini 3. Related to UFO phenomena, clear and glitter-like "nests," also called spider strings. (See below.)

    1. Delicate yarn used for knitting or other craft projects.

    2a. Recipe with angel hair pasta:

Capellini with Herb Spinach,
as printed in *Light and Easy Diabetes Cuisine*, by Betty Marks

Ingredients:
    8 oz angel hair pasta (capellini)
    10 oz pack frozen spinach *or*
    1 lb fresh spinach
    1 tablespoon virgin olive oil
    1 onion, chopped
    2 tablespoons fresh parsley, chopped
    ½ teaspoon dried leaf basil
    ½ teaspoon dried leaf oregano
    ½ teaspoon ground nutmeg
    Salt and pepper to taste
    2 tablespoons grated Parmesan cheese

Bring a large kettle of water to a boil and cook pasta until al dente, 3 minutes. Drain in a colander and set aside. Meanwhile place frozen spinach in a steamer rack over boiling water until slightly wilted. In a nonstick skillet, heat oil and sauté onion until softened. Place spinach, parsley, basil, oregano, nutmeg, salt, and pepper in a blender or a food processor fitted with metal blade and process to purée. Place pasta in a serving bowl and toss with sauce. Sprinkle with Parmesan cheese.

2b. Brands of angel hair pasta, available at most fine grocery stores:

1. Agnesi Capelli d'Angelo
2. Agnesi Cappellini
3. Barilla Angel Hair
4. De Cecco Capellini
5. Deboles Organic Artichoke Angel Hair
6. Deboles Organic Whole Wheat Angel Hair
7. Ronzoni Capellini

3. Related to superstring theory in physics in terms of patterning, these mysterious "webs" are associated with UFO sightings as well as angel sightings. Those who believe in UFOs believe the white filamentlike threads are related to the source that powers UFOs, while skeptics believe the filaments come from balloon spiders or a related spider family.

ANGELOLOGY: The study of angels. This specific field of study is one of the nine major categories of theological study. The other areas include bibliology, anthropology, ecclesiology, theology proper, Christology, soteriology, pneumatology, and eschatology.

ANGELS FLIGHT FUNICULAR RAILWAY: Constructed in 1901, the Angels Flight Funicular Railway was a vertical transport experiment headed by Colonel J. W. Eddy of Los Angeles. The railway covered a short but steep incline named Bunker Hill, which is only 315 feet high but boasts a daunting 33 percent grade incline. Two cars, named "Olivet" and "Sinai," shuttled people up and down the hill for many years, until the 1960s. The railway was restored in 1996 but was then shut down in 2001 after an accident on the railway killed one person and injured seven.

FEAST OF GUARDIAN ANGELS: An event held in honor of guardian angels, this feast was officially put on the Catholic Church's general calendar by Paul V in 1608.

BLUE ANGELS: Founded in 1946, the Blue Angels are a team of expert stunt pilots from the U.S. Navy and Marine Corps.
See Blue Devils, page 95

THE ANGELIC ALPHABET: Actually, "Angel Alphabet" is a term describing many (plural) alphabet systems used to communicate with angels. These alphabets are attributed to various angels or sources, though their true origins/creators often remain unknown. Also called "eye writing," the specific angel alphabet systems are distinguished by names including Celestial Writing, Passing Through the River, Malachim, and Theban.

THE ANGELS, BASEBALL TEAM: Founded in 1960, the Angels played as the Los Angeles Angels from 1961 through 1964, and as the California Angels from 1965–1996, before adopting their present name of Anaheim Angels. The team played its first game against the Baltimore Orioles on April 11, 1961. Highlights include a near miss playing the 1986 World Series, and in 2003 the team became the first major sports team to be owned by a Latino man or woman. Their new owner, Arturo Moreno, bought the team on May 15. From the birth of the Angels until his own death, actor and singer Gene Autry owned the team (he died on October 2, 1998). Although the Dodgers were the first Major League team in Los Angeles, the Angels were the first American League team in California. As the California Angels, the team was one of only six now-active teams ever to use a state in its name. (Other teams include the Twins, Rangers, Rockies, Marlins, and Diamondbacks.) The team won the American League Championship and the World Series in 2002. Angels Hall of Famers include: Reggie Jackson, Rod Carew, Frank Robinson, Nolan Ryan, Don Sutton, Hoyt Wilhelm, and Dave Winfield.

BEHEADING THE ANGEL-MAN: A German tradition observed through the early twentieth century. The angel-man was made of a stump wrapped in straw, with a clumsy human form similar to a scarecrow. The angel-man was lit to celebrate the summer solstice and young boys would attack the burning figure and jump over the remnants of the fire.

ANGEL WREATHS/FEATHER CROWNS: Perhaps from the same original folklore come two different beliefs: 1) the formation of a feather crown as a good omen and 2) the reward of feather crowns by angels. In the first case, people believed that when the feathers inside those down pillows belonging to the deceased formed into clumps, or "wreaths" of feathers, the deceased person (owner of the "clumpy pillow") was on his or her way to heaven. In the second case, people believed that when a person dies, angels descend and sew a crown or wreaths of feathers from the deceased person's pillow. Most likely, polyfil alternatives are available or will be shortly.

Persian devil

Turkish devil

THE LUCIFERIAN LEXICON

HELLHOUND: A dog from hell, such as Cerberus, or slang for an evil person. See *Hellkite*.

HELL-MOTH: In the Dungeons and Dragons world, a hell-moth is a giant moth that attempts to overtake victims with its wings and then self-immolate.

HELLKITE: A cruel person.

HELL BROTH: A magical potion used for evil purposes. It appears in *Macbeth* IV, i.

HELL GATES: Term derived from Milton's *Paradise Lost*, in one of his most famous allegorical passages. Milton writes of nine Hell Gates, controlled by keepers Sin and Death.

HELLHOLE: An unpleasant, repellant place.

HELLFIRE: The punishment of heat and fire in hell.

HELL'S HEMI: A 1965 Belvedere.

HELL'S KITCHEN: Home of the Civil War draft riots, Hell's Kitchen is an area of New York City bound by Eighth Avenue and the Hudson River, from 34th Street to 59th Street. Real estate agents now prefer to call the area Clinton or "Midtown West."

HELL, RICHARD: Born in 1949, Richard Hell was a poet before joining musician Tom Verlaine to form the Neon Boys, later renamed Television. He eventually broke off and in the mid-seventies was considered a defining figure of the punk movement. After his 1984 album, *RIP,* he left the music business, but he briefly returned to it to record an album with two members of Sonic Youth and one member of the band Gumball. He continues to publish as a poet and novelist.

HELL'S HUNDRED ACRES: Now one of the most famous and expensive neighborhoods in New York City, Soho, or "South of Houston," was once called "Hell's Hundred Acres" over one hundred years ago, at the turn of the nineteenth century. The name came from the epidemic of fires that plagued the area once it transitioned from an upper-class residential neighborhood to a place filled with factories. As the area quickly became the city's red-light district, its factories, made of wooden floors and beams, frequently caught on fire, inspiring the name Hell's Hundred Acres.

DEVIL'S TRIANGLE: Also known as the Bermuda Triangle, the Devil's Triangle is an area of the Atlantic Ocean over which various aircraft, ships, and people have mysteriously disappeared. This area is bounded by three geographic points: Miami; Bermuda; and Puerto Rico. Theories of why so many people have been lost in this one area include proposed unfriendly extraterrestrials, evil humans with special antigravity devices, and "oceanic flatulence" (gas release). In 1945, five U.S. Navy planes disappeared over the area, inspiring a modern fascination with a historic mystery. This fascination was nurtured by several quasi-literary works, including an article by George X. Sands in a 1952 issue of *Fate* magazine; a book entitled *Limbo of the Lost* by John Wallace Spencer (1969); and the best-selling *The Bermuda Triangle* by Charles Berlitz (1974).

THE JERSEY DEVIL: During the past 260 years, more than 2,000 witnesses claimed to have seen the Jersey Devil. Many towns profess

to be the birthplace of the mysterious "beast," offering various myths
to explain its birth. Though the sightings began as early as the 1800s
and for the most part dwindled by 1903, a thousand people reported
seeing what is now called the Jersey Devil over the course of one
week in 1909. Described as a "birdlike creature with a horse's head"
by one witness, the Jersey Devil reportedly left hoofprints in its wake.
Several witnesses saw it fly and heard it scream. Descriptions continued to amass, slowly forming an amalgamated three-and-a-half-
foot beast with a collie dog's face and a horse's head, plus the legs of
a crane and the feet of a horse. So many people reported simultaneous sightings of the Jersey Devil during that one particular week
in 1909 that schools and factories shut down. One professor believes
the Jersey Devil must be some kind of pterodactyl. The Jersey Devil,
according to these sightings, has already outlived any bird, even a
rare species. One of the most outrageous alternate explanations for
the beast is a story of a woman who locked up her deformed child in
an attic until it starved and flew out the chimney. *The X-Files* based
one of its episode's plot lines on this mysterious beast and this un-
likely explanation.

DUST DEVILS: Wind phenomena that are similar to (but less powerful
than) tornadoes. The diameter of a typical dust devil is anywhere
between 10 and 300 feet. Dust devils form from extremely hot surfaces, particularly where two different types of heated surfaces meet
(asphalt and sand, for example). More recently, dust devils have been
spotted on the surface of Mars.

TAMPA BAY DEVIL RAYS: In 1995 this baseball team was added to the
roster of Major League teams, along with the Arizona Diamondbacks,
signing a thirty-year lease with the city of St. Petersburg, Florida,
to play all home games at the Thunderdome Stadium. Both teams
began playing in 1998.

DEVIL PODS or BAT NUTS: Devil pods, also called bat nuts or goat heads,
are seedpods from an aquatic Asian plant called *Trapa bicornis.*
They're called devil pods, among other things, because the pod looks,
from a certain angle, like a horned demon. Some people use the seedpods to ward off evil, though the insides are edible, if cooked.

Heaven and Hell

TASMANIAN DEVIL: This small, distinct beast, also known as *Sarcophilus harrisii*, is the world's largest surviving carnivorous marsupial. Named a "devil" for its black color, hideous screeching, and nasty temperament, this animal is found only in Tasmania, though many believe it was once present throughout Europe. The Tasmanian devil's disappearance from Europe is attributed to the dingo's ferocity. In addition to its black coloring, the devil is sometimes speckled with patches of white. A large, male devil weighs approximately 12 kilograms, and is approximately 2 feet, or 60 centimeters, long. Physical comparisons have been made of the Tasmanian devil to a small bear. The devils thrive in both dry forest or rain forest, basically any habitat where they can hide during the day and scavenge for food at night. Bugs Bunny fans will remember the wily ways of the animated Tasmanian devil, or "Taz," as he hounded Bugs, moving in the form of a tornado and slobbering when still. What Taz fans may not know is that his character was banned briefly from television by producer Ed Selzer in 1954. The ban followed the release of a Taz episode titled "Devil May Hare." Jack Warner himself, however, missed Taz and requested him back on the screen in 1957. In 1991 Taz briefly had a cartoon of his own, *Taz-Mania*, which portrayed the slobbering tornado-beast as a family man.

DEVIL'S TOENAILS: Also known as *gryphaea*, these former seabed dwellers are an extinct type of oyster. They once lived in large colonies and now exist as fossils, dating back to the Jurassic and Triassic periods.

DEVIL'S NIGHT: The name of a quasi-holiday, "celebrated" on the eve of Halloween. Most infamous in the state of Michigan—specifically in Detroit—Devil's Night is an occasion, historically, for numerous acts of violence as well as incidents involving arson and vandalism. Some years, more than three hundred fires have been set in Detroit on Devil's Night. Over five years ago, the city of Detroit tried to initiate a countermovment called "Angel's Night," with mixed success. Several thousand volunteers now patrol Detroit streets on Devil's Night.

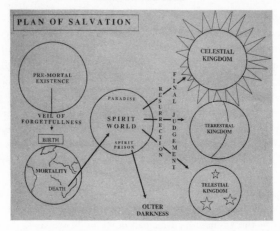

THE MORMON PLAN OF SALVATION

According to the Mormon faith, God created this plan of salvation so humans could gain entry to present-day life in a physical body, accumulating these experiences in order to become more "God-like." According to this scheme, those who adhere to the teachings of the church will ultimately return to God, at which point they can potentially become God-like and populate their own planets.

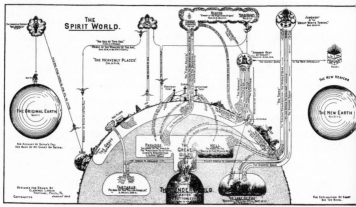

The Spirit World, Clarence Larkin

ANGELS FOR THE DAYS OF THE WEEK

Day	Angel	Ideal Activities for Day
Monday	Gabriel	Divulging secrets, finding silver
Tuesday	Samuel	Starting wars and fires
Wednesday	Raphael	Teaching science experiments, opening locks, improving health
Thursday	Sachiel	Wooing the ladies, finding lost items
Friday	Anael	Inspiring marriage, finding silver
Saturday	Cassiel	Murdering, planting evil thoughts
Sunday	Michael	Finding and receiving forgiveness

ANGEL-OF-THE-MONTH CLUB, NOT YOUR AVERAGE PINUP CALENDAR

Month	Angel
January	Gabriel
February	Barchiel
March	Malchidiel
April	Asmodel
May	Ambriel
June	Muriel
July	Verchiel
August	Hamliel
September	Uriel
October	Barbiel
November	Adnachiel
December	Anael

ANGELS OF THE SEASONS

(according to Rudolf Steiner*)

Season	Angel
Winter	Gabriel
Spring	Raphael
Summer	Uriel
Autumn	Michael

*Rudolf Steiner (1861–1925) was an educator, philosopher, and founder of Anthroposophy.

ANGELS OF THE PLANETS

	Angel Islam	According to Occult
Sun	Michael	Semeliel
Moon	Gabriel	Jareahel
Mercury	Raphael	Cochabiel
Venus	Anael	Nogahel
Mars	Samael	Madimiel
Jupiter	Zadkiel	Zedekiel
Saturn	Cassiel	Sabathiel

WET YOUR WHISTLE: THE HELLION'S HAIR-OF-THE-DOG

(also known as The Devil's Cocktail)

Combine:
½ part port
½ part dry vermouth
2 dashes lemon juice
Stir well with ice and strain into glasses

Heaven and Hell

The Trinity of Evil: from a French manuscript,
fifteenth century. Reprinted in *Iconography*, by A. N. Didron

SPIRITUAL HIERARCHIES
According to Rudolf Steiner's Scheme,
with Angels Bridging Earth and Heaven

(Listed from Bottom to Top)

Earth	3rd Hierarchy	2nd Hierarchy	1st Hierarchy	Heaven
				Father
				Son
				Holy Ghost
			Seraphim	
			Cherubim	
			Thrones/Spirits	
		Spirits of Motion		
		Spirits of Wisdom		
		Spirits of Form, Creators		
	Spirits of the Age (Zeitgeist)			
	Archangels			
	Angels			
	(Guiding Spirits)			
Man				
Animals				
Plants				
Minerals				

See angel hierarchy, page 9
See Angels of the Seasons, page 66

The Great Triumphal Car by Albrecht Dürer. The cardinal virtues are
portrayed here as passengers and guides. The car is guided by Reason,
while Fortitude and Prudence stand on two pedestals.

See virtues, page 25

TERMS FOR HELL IN THE BIBLE

1. A PIT: Rev. 9:1 (a bottomless pit)
2. ABADDON: Rev. 9:11. A Hebrew word found in the Wisdom litera-
   ture of the Old Testament denoting *the place of the lost* (Job 26:6)
3. APOLLYON: *Destroyer*, a Greek translation of the Hebrew word
   Abaddon, or destruction: in Rev. 9:11; it is the name of the Angel of
   the Abyss (bottomless pit) made familiar to English readers of
   Bunyan's *Pilgrim's Progress*
4. DESTRUCTION: Matt. 7:13
5. EVERLASTING FIRE: Matt. 13:42
6. EXTERIOR DARKNESS (Outer Darkness): Matt. 22:13

7. FURNACE OF FIRE: Rev. 20:10
8. LOWER HELL: lower parts of the earth: Eph. 4:9
9. MIST OF DARKNESS: 2 Pet. 2:17
10. PERDITION: Rev. 17:8
11. PLACE OF FIRE AND BRIMSTONE: Rev. 20:10
12. PLACE OF TORMENTS: Luke 16:28
13. UNQUENCHABLE FIRE: Mark 9:43 ". . . the fire that never shall be quenched."
14. BLACKNESS OF DARKNESS: Jude 1:13

Descriptions of Hell in the Bible— Can You See It?

1. A FIERY LAKE: (Rev. 19:20)
2. INSIDE THE EARTH: Theologians argue where, exactly, hell is. According to a few places in the Bible, hell may be located inside earth; the earth opens and the wicked fall in and sink.

See Dante's Inferno, *page 100*

Typical conception of hell,
German woodcut from the age of Reformation

HEAVENLY MOVIES: PARADISIACAL PLOTS

DAYS OF HEAVEN (1978): In this Terrence Malick film, released in 1978, Richard Gere and Brooke Adams deliver an exquisitely torturous love story against a bucolic landscape. Nestor Almendros, the film's cinematographer, won an Oscar for his work. Sometimes called the "J. D. Salinger of film," Malick maintains an uncharacteristically low profile for an acclaimed Hollywood director/producer.

Why Filming Terrence Malick's *Days of Heaven* Was Not Heavenly

1. Nestor Almendros, the film's cinematographer, was slowly going blind during production. Each day, his assistant took Polaroid photographs of the scenes, which Almendros would review the following day with the assistance of a powerful magnifying glass.
2. After production began, Malick boldly trashed the script and filmed the actors' improvisations for over a year.
3. Malick stubbornly insisted on filming during the "golden" hours between day and night, which occur extremely early in the morning or late at night.
4. In this film, three shots come out of a double-barreled shotgun (ouch).

HEAVEN HELP US (1985): This coming-of-age film takes place at an all-boys' Catholic school in Brooklyn, New York, circa 1965. With a star-studded cast, including Donald Sutherland, Mary Stuart Masterson, Andrew McCarthy, and Wallace Shawn, this film struck a chord with any misfit who's roamed a school's halls. In U.S. rentals alone, the film grossed $2,700,000 in profits.

HEAVEN KNOWS, MR. ALLISON (1957): With a premise that is just perverse enough to work as soft porn (were that the writer's/director's intention), the film chronicles a quasi–love story between a Marine corporal and an Irish nun, who are stranded on a remote island together. Ultimately, the girl chooses God.

HEAVEN'S GATE (1980): Michael Cimino's multimillion-dollar flop was ultimately the cause of the United Artists studio's collapse and sale to MGM. More than 1.5 million feet of film were used to tell a story based in Wyoming, in the 1890s, of star-crossed love, immigrant life, and the western frontier. The film was off to a rough start when Cimino rejected the set designed to his own specifications and decided to raze both sides of the "street" and rebuild it for $1.2 million. By day five of filming, the production was four days behind.

HEAVEN CAN WAIT (1978): Directed by Warren Beatty, this strange film chronicles a successful quarterback (Rams) who's accidentally sent to heaven, only to be returned to earth in the body of a recently murdered millionaire. If pressed to identify this film's niche, it would have to be placed alongside *Freaky Friday* and other favorite body-swapping films. Fun facts about the film include Beatty's original intention to make the quarterback a boxer instead, with the idea that Muhammad Ali would be Beatty's first choice for the role. Beatty himself starred instead, along with Julie Christie. This film grossed $49,400,000 in U.S. rentals. Not to be confused with *Heaven Can Wait* of 1943 (see below).

HEAVEN CAN WAIT (1943): In this religious drama based on a play titled *Birthdays*, our protagonist arrives at the gates of hell, but the gates do not readily open. The protagonist then narrates the numerous wrongs he's committed against women—adultery and womanizing, among others—a list that constitutes the film's plot.

FAR FROM HEAVEN (2002): Written and directed by Todd Haynes, this film offers a dark take on domestic affairs in the 1950s, exploring both the sexual and racial taboos of the Donna Reed era. Starring Julianne Moore, Dennis Quaid, and Patricia Clarkson, this film was nominated for multiple Academy Awards, in the categories of Best Actress (Moore), Best Cinematography, Best Music, and Best Writing.

GATES OF HEAVEN (1978): In this brilliant documentary, director Errol Morris explores a pet cemetery in California, probing the cemetery as well as the pet owners who use it.

SEVEN MINUTES IN HEAVEN (1986): One of the all-time greatest teenage flicks, this film chronicles the heartaches and growing pains of three fifteen-year-olds. Starring a young Jennifer Connelly, this film did not do as well by its other stars (Byron Thames and Maddie Corman), who now dwell in obscurity.

PENNIES FROM HEAVEN (1936): Though more famous for the title song from its sound track than for its story, this original film's plot is quite different from the 1981 remake. In this incarnation, also a musical, two prisoners strike a deal. One inmate, sentenced to death, asks another inmate, soon to be released, to compensate the victims of his violent crime by leaving them his estate. Miraculously, this film works as both a comedy and a musical, despite the potentially heavy plot.

PENNIES FROM HEAVEN (1978): Released in Great Britain as a television series, this show garnered awards for Best Actor (Bob Hoskins), Actress (Cheryl Campbell), and Film Editor (David Martin).

PENNIES FROM HEAVEN (1981): In this second remake of the original, a sheet music salesman struggles to sell his wares, defeated with his lack of sales and stagnant home life until he falls in love with another woman. Steve Martin, Bernadette Peters, and Christopher Walken star in this romantic depression-era musical. While the film's budget approached $22,000,000, it grossed only $3,600,000.

Other Heaven/Angel Movies

WINGS OF DESIRE (1988) • CITY OF ANGELS (1998)
ANGEL ON MY SHOULDER (1946) • DATE WITH AN ANGEL (1987)

HELLISH MOVIES: FLICKS ON THE STYX

ROSEMARY'S BABY (1968): Directed by Roman Polanski, this campy horror film centers around a newly married couple, Rosemary and Guy Woodhouse (Mia Farrow and John Cassavetes). After several strange occurrences, Rosemary, newly pregnant, begins to believe a Satanic cult is after her and her unborn child. Alfred Hitchcock was originally slated to direct this film, though Polanski obviously did well by it: the film was nominated for two Oscars and won one of them (Best Supporting Actress for Ruth Gordon), while accruing multiple nominations and awards from other competitions.

BILL & TED'S BOGUS JOURNEY (1991): Bill and Ted are threatened by their evil doubles (robots) and must, simply put, meet God, escape hell, and dupe the Grim Reaper, all to make it back to earth for the Battle of the Bands.

DEVIL'S ISLAND (1940): Dr. Gaudet, a brain surgeon, is exiled to a brutal penal colony (Devil's Island) after offering medical treatment to a revolutionary.

FROM HELL (2001): Set in London during the late nineteenth century, this film is both a love story and a murder mystery. The plot centers on the historic search for Jack the Ripper, and one investigator's love for a prostitute whom he aims to protect.

JASON GOES TO HELL: THE FINAL FRIDAY (1993): Supposedly the last of the Jason series, Jason has the power in this movie to become any person he touches. Despite his changing shape, his motive is finally revealed.

GO TO HELL! (1997): Though many movie lovers might have missed it, this strange film centers around the absurd notion that "God" is not a spirit or deity but is instead an alien that wiped out the dinosaurs. The devil (or "little red") is the alien's son and disrupts the alien's plans throughout time (now history).

MOTEL HELL (1980): Both a comedy and a horror flick, the premise of this film is a quasi-satire of so many horror flicks you may vaguely remember but not be able to name. Farmer Vincent plans to sell his victims as food at his roadside stand. His motto: "It takes all kinds of critters...to make Farmer Vincent Fritters."

NO EXIT (1962): Based on a play by Jean-Paul Sartre, the plot is simple: Three people are led to a room and slowly realize they've entered hell, with no way out (hence the title). From this movie comes the famous Sartre line, "Hell is other people!"

HIGHWAY TO HELL (1992): In this film, prisoners on the road are taken to hell instead of prison. A woman is kidnapped from the road to be Satan's bride. Don't miss: the road of good intentions.

MONSTER FROM GREEN HELL (1957): An extraterrestrial of the emerald-colored persuasion visits planet earth.

FROM HELL IT CAME (1957): Oddly enough, this sci-fi film offers something new. A killer reincarnated as (yes, that's right) a walking tree stump. Ultimately, the stump comes back to life and murders several people before heroic scientists nab the former killer-cum-stump.

ROCK 'N' ROLL NIGHTMARE (1987): When a heavy metal band named The Tritons descends upon a farmhouse to work on their craft, strange things begin to happen. Ultimately, the death of a family on the same property haunts the band until only one member is left standing.

FROM *THE MARRIAGE OF HEAVEN AND HELL* BY WILLIAM BLAKE, PLATE 3

As a new heaven is begun, and it is now thirty-three years since its advent: the Eternal Hell revives. And lo! Swedenborg is the Angel sitting at the tomb; his writings are the linen clothes folded up. Now is the dominion of Edom, & the return of Adam into Paradise; see Isaiah XXXIV & XXXV Chap: Without Contraries is no progression. Attraction and Repulsion, Reason and Energy, Love and Hate, are necessary to Human existence.

From these contraries spring what the religious call Good & Evil. Good is the passive that obeys Reason[.] Evil is the active springing from Energy.

Good is Heaven. Evil is Hell.

Composed of three spirals, the triskele is a Celtic symbol related to reincarnation and the afterlife. Composed with one continuous line, the design suggests eternity and continuity.

Sometimes called "Hrungnir's heart," the valknut is most
likely a symbol of the afterlife. The symbol's nine points
reference the nine worlds of Norse mythology.
See Norse Mythology and Its Nine Worlds, page 107

COCKTAIL BREAK:
THE GATES OF HELL

2 oz tequila
a dash of lemon juice
a dash of lime juice
a dash of cherry brandy

Combine, shake on ice, and strain. Serve in an old-
fashioned glass. Drizzle extra cherry brandy over the top.

DEVAS AND THE SEVEN SEPHIROT

Devas are recognized in both the Hindi and Buddhist religions as well
as in the practice of Theosophy. In the Hindu religion, devas are either: 1) elevated mortals; 2) enlightened humans; or 3) Brahman, as a
personal God. The Buddhist religion, however, views devas as gods
occupying various realms of the heavens as a reward for their goodness,
yet even these devas go through the process of reincarnation. From a
Theosophical perspective, devas are more like angels.

THE FIRST SEPHIRA: Filled with devas called the Morning Stars, the first sephira is responsible for orchestrating creation and transforming energy and/or will into the material world.

THE SECOND SEPHIRA: Responsible for harmony, these devas are also known as the "Sound of Wisdom." Specifically, they also deal with balance in harmony in nature.

THE THIRD SEPHIRA: These "Sons of Intelligence" give birth to other devas (less significant in terms of the hierarchy).

THE FOURTH SEPHIRA: This fourth order of devas connects the highest (see above) three orders with the secondary orders (see below).

THE FIFTH SEPHIRA: Highly complex, this fifth order is the "soul" of the third order.

THE SIXTH SEPHIRA: Represented by both air and water, this order of devas is related to the second order. Just as the fifth order is related to the third, the sixth order is related to the second; these devas comprise the actual substance of which nature is made.

THE SEVENTH SEPHIRA: This last group of devas is represented by earth, and these devas or angels are responsible for making and maintaining all matter on earth.

For further reading, see The Encyclopedia of Angels *by Rosemary Ellen Guiley*

WET YOUR WHISTLE: SATANIC SIP

(also known as The Devil)

Combine:
    2/3 jigger brandy
    2/3 jigger green crème de menthe
    1 pinch red pepper

Shake brandy and crème de menthe and strain into glass. Sprinkle with red pepper.

PLACES: THE ASCENDANT ALMANAC

ANGEL FALLS: The world's highest waterfall (3,212 feet), in Venezuela.

ANGEL ISLAND: Island in San Francisco Bay, California, that contains a former immigration detention center.

BLUE HEAVEN OSTRICH RANCH, NORTH CAROLINA: Madeleine Calder, president of the Ostrich Ranch, manufactures genuine ostrich products here, including ostrich ravioli, ostrich burgers, ostrich hot dogs ("Birdogs"), and ostrich steaks.

HEAVEN'S GATE NATIONAL RECREATION TRAIL (Idaho): Along this trail is a lookout with a view of four states (Washington, Oregon, Idaho, and Montana), and an overlook of Hell's Canyon. Other highlights include alpine wildflowers and various peaks. See Hell's Canyon, She Devil Peak, He Devil Peak, and the Seven Devils.

HEAVEN'S PEAK: Mountain in Glacier National Park, northwest Montana (9,008 feet).

PARADISE, MICHIGAN: A mere one hour from Michigan's Mackinac Bridge, Paradise is a shoreline town, equipped to deal with heavy tourism. Among its offerings are bird-watching, camping, fishing, and (in the winter) cross-country skiing and snowmobiling.

PLACES: DEMONIC DETOURS

DEVIL'S ISLAND: On the north coast of French Guiana this served as a penal colony for the French during the later half of the nineteenth

Heaven and Hell

century. Alfred Dreyfus was a prisoner here (1895). Penal colonies were abolished in 1938.

DEVIL'S LAKE, NORTH DAKOTA: Located in the northeastern region of North Dakota, this lake is especially rich with walleye and northern pike.

DEVIL'S TOWER NATIONAL MONUMENT: Established by President Theodore Roosevelt in 1906, this monument is a tourist destination. Rock climbers like to test their skills on the monument's near-vertical walls.

HELLFIRE PASS: Also known as *Halfaya* Pass, this area in northwestern Egypt was the site of heavy fighting in World War II.

HELL GATE: Called a *Hoellgat* (whirling gut) by New Yorkers, this is a narrow part of the East River, between New York City and Long Island. It's partially spanned by the Hell Gate Bridge.

HELL HOLE BAY WILDERNESS, SOUTH CAROLINA: 2,125 acres of wilderness managed by the U.S. Forest Service, made up of (mostly) swamps and wetlands. Snakes (water moccasins, copperheads, and rattlesnakes) inhabit the area, along with the endangered red-cockaded woodpecker.

HELL HOLE RESERVOIR, CALIFORNIA: Formed by a dam built in 1966 by the Bureau of Reclamation for irrigation, this reservoir is used for irrigation, power generation, water supply, and recreation. Desolation Valley Wilderness is situated nearby. (You can't accuse anyone of seductive advertising strategies here.)

HELL, MICHIGAN: Livingston County. Various explanations exist for the town's name. It might have been named by two German visitors, who said "Hell" when they arrived, meaning (in German) "bright and beautiful." On the other hand, it's possible that early travelers were struck by the darkness and wetness of the town, sitting low beneath the main trail they would have traveled. The associations of darkness and wetness with hell might have inspired the settlers to name the town as such.

HELL'S CANYON: Formerly the deepest canyon in the United States, located along the Idaho/Oregon border.

78

PLACES: NOT SURE WHICH WAY TO GO?

PURGATORY CHASM (Middletown), RHODE ISLAND: This small strip of state park looks out onto the ocean. Those who tire of the view can amble along several nature trails. This chasm was actually created by erosion from the sea.

PURGATORY, COLORADO: Located between the towns of Silverton and Durango, Purgatory is a "hot spot" for skiers and snowboarders. Purgatory's summit elevation is 10,822 feet and its base elevation is 8,793 feet; that's a 2,029-foot drop.

SEVEN LODGES OF HELL (OR ARKA) IN THE KABBALAH

Key: [A] heat; [B] who goes there; [C] presiding angel

1. Gehennom
   - A. It "snows fire" here. The heat is sixty times hotter than fire
   - B. Israelites who break the law, and Absalom
   - C. Kushiel

2. The Gates of Death
   - A. The heat is sixty times hotter than number 1
   - B. Doeg
   - C. Labatiel

3. The Shadow of Death
   - A. The heat is sixty times hotter than number 2
   - B. Korah
   - C. Shaftiel

4. The Pit of Corruption
   - A. The heat is sixty times hotter than number 3
   - B. Jeroboam
   - C. Maccathiel

5. The Mire of Clay
    A. The heat is sixty times hotter than number 4
    B. Ahab
    C. Chutriel

6. Abaddon
    A. The heat is sixty times hotter than number 5
    B. Micah
    C. Pasiel

7. Sheol
    A. The heat is sixty times hotter than number 6, or 420 times hotter than fire
    B. Sabbath breakers, idolators, and those uncircumsized
    C. Dalkiel

SEVEN HELLS OF THE MUHAMMADANS

1. Jabannam .... for sinful Muhammadans, who will all eventually be taken to Paradise
2. The Flamer (Latha) .... for Christians
3. The Smasber (Hutamah) .... for Jews
4. The Blazer Sair .... for Sabians
5. The Scorcher (Sakar) .... for Magians
6. The Burner (Johim) .... for idolaters
7. The Abyss (Hawiyah) .... for hypocrites

See Seven Heavens of the Muhammadans, page 49

THE NINE ORDERS OF DEMONS

(According to the Pseudo-Dionysius Hierarchy)

1. FALSE GODS: Ruled by Beelzebub, these false gods become the object of worship.
2. SPIRITS OF LIES: Ruled by Pytho, the spirits of lies fool those in charge of delivering truth, such as prophets and diviners.
3. VESSELS OF WRATH: Ruled by Belial, these beings invent "wicked" gambling junkets and card games.
4. REVENGERS OF EVIL: Ruled by Asmodeus, these beings are responsible for all poor judgment.
5. DELUDERS: Ruled by Satan, these beings orchestrate false yet persuasive miracles.
6. AERIAL POWERS: Responsible for pestilence, these beings attach themselves to thunder and lightning.
7. FURIES: Ruled by Abaddon, furies are responsible for war and violence.
8. ACCUSERS: Ruled by Astaroth, these beings—what else but—lie and falsely accuse.
9. TEMPTERS AND ENSNARERS: Ruled by mammon, these beings incite jealousy.

See The Nine Orders of Angels, page 9

COMPARATIVE COSMOGRAPHY AND ESCHATOLOGY

ESCHATOLOGY: The doctrine of last or final things (i.e., death) and the judgment related to these things. Comes from *escot*, which means "last," and *logos*, which means "discourse."

SCIENTOLOGY: Based entirely on the writings and philosophy of science-fiction author L. Ron Hubbard, this religion is most famous for its celebrity adherents. Scientologists do not believe in heaven and hell, or original sin. Scientology does uphold a belief in reincarnation, and Scientologists do believe that each person experiences personal salvation by cleansing oneself of "destructive" memories and experiences.

BAHA'I: Most significantly a humanist religion, the Baha'i faith is concerned with uniting all faiths, prophets, and people. Not surprisingly, the United Nations is enthusiastic about this religion. Baha'i grew out of Islam but unlike the Muslim belief in Muhammad as the great prophet, followers of Baha'i believe the second coming will be indicated by the arrival of the prophet Baha'u'llah. On the subject of sin, Baha'i faith states (unlike Christianity) that humans are imperfect but not "fallen" in sin. Heaven and hell, in this faith, are not regarded as geographic places but rather "states," or conditions. "Heaven" is a place close to God whereas "Hell" is a place far away from God. Details of the afterlife are vague in the Baha'i faith though members believe and are told it will be wonderful. Present life on earth is seen as a place and time to gather/hone tools for the afterlife, comparable to the time a baby spends in a mother's womb before birth. Ultimately, when Judgment Day occurs, followers of the Baha'i faith believe that each person will have the opportunity to believe in this message or not, and to follow the messenger, or choose not to follow.

ISLAM: Less specific on the details of "end time" than the Bible, the Koran does explicate a vision of end time in which the earth is leveled, and men and women will stand waiting for judgment from Allah. In addition to the Koran, the hadith, which is a collection of expressions of the Prophet Muhammad, passed down through oral tradition, also offers a few more details, including signs of the imminent end time. Male martyrs will go to Paradise, where Allah will grant them seventy-two females, who remain perpetual virgins. Others argue the number is seventy.

EGYPTIAN HEAVEN AND HELL: Ancient Egyptian religion described a sought-after afterlife as one spent eternally with Osiris, the sun god and resident of the underworld. The dead were called the "living," and the coffin was called the "chest of the living," while the tomb was called the "lord of life." The soul continues to live after death, though this specific conception of soul allows for some bodily functions and organs. According to Egyptian tradition, as detailed in the Book of the Dead (chapter 125), the "living" must be able to answer to forty-two categories of sin, and deny any indulgence in these sins. Ultimately, each person's heart is weighed against truth and justice. Entry to any type of heaven or hell is not immediate. After a commendatory judgment, a person still must face many obstacles before reaching Aalu, comparable to the paradise and heaven envisioned in other faiths. To navigate their way through these obstacles, the "living" must use lessons and skills acquired in life, along with the support of friends from earth. Egyptian eschatology does not expand upon the fate of those who fail to navigate this path, though terms such as "second death" are present and might mean the ultimate failure to exist in any form, though it's possible failure is punished according to the degree of failure, as success or "blessing" is also rewarded according to degree.

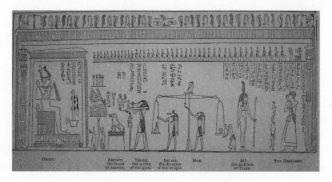

The weighing of the heart in the Hall of Truth,
from Lepsius's reproduction of the Turin papyrus.

GREEK: According to ancient Greek tradition, life is the highest reward and death is viewed as a punishment. According to this tradition, a person exists after his or her death as a shade, or psyche. Life as a shade appears boring and unimportant according to Greek epic poems. Exceptionally evil or corrupt psyches were sent to Tartarus (*see Tartarus, page 5*), the lowest hell, and exceptionally beloved psyches were sent by the gods to Elysian Fields (*see Elysian Fields, page 3*). Later in Greek tradition (after the Homeric era), a distinction was made between Tartarus and the less severe punishment of Acherusian Lake, or one may stay only temporarily at Tartarus, for the purpose of penance.

CATHOLIC: The Catholic tradition holds that a soul is separated from its physical body at the time of death and that each person's fate is decided or judged at that time. The three possibilities, in terms of destinies for each soul, are: heaven, hell, or purgatory. Heaven is defined as a place for the blessed, and also as the abode of God, the angels, and Christ. Purgatory is the destination offered for those who fall in between blessed and sinful. In purgatory, these in-between souls are given a chance to purify themselves in preparation for entry into heaven. Hell is the place of eternal punishment for those who've committed personal, mortal sin and/or died with "only original sin on their souls" (*Catholic Encyclopedia*). Ultimately, a new heaven and earth will replace the present heaven and earth.

ANCIENT BABYLONIAN: In this tradition, focus was placed on mortal life. Good deeds or bad deeds were dealt with in earthly life, as humans were rewarded or punished with gifts or curses. Babylonians believed in a ghostlike spirit, ekimmu, that joins the underworld after the physical body is buried. Scholars have found little to no proof of anything describing a blissful heavenlike place.

ANCIENT INDIAN: According to this tradition—looking specifically at Vedic tradition—the ruler Yama presides over the kingdom of the dead, distinguishing the realm for the good and the realm for the evil. For those who reach the realm of the good, they can expect feasts and light, while those in the realm of the evil are in "northernmost darkness." Brahman tradition differs slightly. According to Brahmanism, numerous hells and heavens exist for various degrees of saints and sinners, though these are not permanent destinations. Brahma, which is comparable to the essence, or spirit, of the world, contains the answer to salvation in this tradition. Only followers with perfect understanding and adherence to the ways of Brahma are granted a permanent stay in heaven. All others, even those highly observant, may go to heaven but only temporarily, until they are born and die again.

HINDUISM: According to Hindu tradition, the soul of a deceased person is brought back to the world in the form of another person or animal. The specifics of a soul's new form are based on his or her deeds in his/her life. This kind of reincarnation cycle continues until a soul is perfectly cleansed, when it has attained Atma, and joins God and the angels.

JUDAISM: Though details of the afterlife remain vague in Jewish texts, Paradise is mentioned, along with a Day of Judgment. Various schools of Judaism differ on the more specific events regarding resurrection. Though Orthodox Jews believe in a personal messiah who will usher in the messianic age, Conservative Jews are divided. Some Conservative Jews believe in a personal messiah; others believe only in the messianic age or era. Reform Jews believe in the messianic era but most do not believe in a personal messiah. Reconstructionist Jews believe that only humans, not God, can bring about a messianic world, though they do not believe that God alone can inspire a messiah or even a messianic age. All Jews believe that the soul survives physical death. After death, the soul, according to some rabbinical writings, encounters the angel Dumah, Gehenna (purgatory), and Gan Eden (Paradise). One belief states that every time a Jewish person "sins," s/he creates an angel of destruction, and these angels of destruction would potentially face their creators (sinners) in the afterlife. Gehenna, however, is not a permanent residing place; those who pass through are held no longer than twelve months before taking their places in the afterlife, or (in Hebrew) Olam Ha-Ba. A very few—the most evil—do not move on, but the Jewish tradition encompasses multiple interpretations on what, exactly, happens to these souls.

ANCIENT PERSIAN (such as Zoroastrianism or Mazdaism): In this tradition, souls of the dead leave their physical bodies and cross the bridge of Chinvat, the bridge of the Gatherer or Accountant, for three days, while good and evil struggle with these souls. Those who wrestle successfully with evil are sent to paradise, while those who give in to evil are sent to hell. Those who are somewhere in between are held in a neutral place, to wait for the time of the resurrection. According to this tradition, the resurrection will be fifty-seven years long, at the end of which judgment will be cast upon all souls, and the good and evil will be separated from one another. Both groups, however, will travel through a purgatorial fire. The fire will be more painful for the most evil souls passing through it. Finally, the good and evil spirits will rumble, and the good will conquer. After the evil spirits dissolve, so will hell itself.

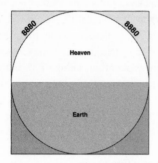

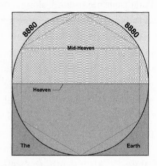

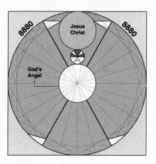

SACRED GEOMETRY BY DANIEL GLEASON: In these unusual diagrams, Gleason offers what he calls a "Gematria-based commentary on the book of Revelation." Based on a complex "code" in which words stand for specific geometric placement, Gleason argues that the geometric representaions form a "cartoon-like strip of moving signs to illustrate the book." Amazingly the various signs from each verse ultimately fit together to form a fully filled-in graph, which Jesus calls 880. Gematria is part of a historical tradition, most often associated with kabbalah. In Hebrew, each Hebrew letter possesses a numerical value. Gematria "calculates" the numerical equivalent of various words, letters, and verses.

HA-HA FOR HELLIONS:
PICK HEAVEN OR HELL

One day while walking down the street, a highly successful woman executive was tragically hit by a bus and she died. Her soul arrived in heaven where she was met at the Pearly Gates by St. Peter himself. "Welcome to Heaven," said St. Peter. "Before you get settled in, though, it seems we have a problem. You see, strangely enough, we've never once had an executive make it this far and we're not really sure what to do with you."

"No problem, just let me in," said the woman.

"Well, I'd like to, but I have higher orders. What we're going to do is let you have a day in Hell and a day in Heaven and then you can choose whichever one you want to spend an eternity in."

"Actually, I think I've made up my mind . . . I prefer to stay in Heaven," said the woman.

"Sorry, we have rules . . ." And with that St. Peter put the executive in an elevator and it went down-down-down to Hell. The doors opened and she found herself stepping out onto the putting green of a beautiful golf course. In the distance was a country club and standing in front of her were all her friends—fellow executives that she had worked with—and they were all dressed in evening gowns and cheering for her. They ran up and kissed her on both cheeks and they talked about old times. They played an excellent round of golf and at night went to the country club where she enjoyed an excellent steak and lobster dinner. She met the Devil who was actually a really nice guy (kinda cute) and she had a great time telling jokes and dancing. She was having such a good time that before she knew it, it was time to leave. Everybody shook her hand and waved good-bye as she got on the elevator.

The elevator went up-up-up and opened back at the Pearly Gates and she found St. Peter waiting for her. "Now it's time to spend a day in Heaven," he said.

So she spent the next twenty-four hours lounging around on clouds and playing the harp and singing. She had a great time and before she knew it her twenty-four hours were up and St. Peter came and got her.

"So, you've spent a day in Hell and you've spent a day in Heaven. Now you must choose your eternity," he said.

The woman paused for a second and then replied, "Well, I never thought I'd say this, I mean, Heaven has been really great and all, but I think I had a better time in Hell."

So St. Peter escorted her to the elevator and again she went down-down-down back to Hell. When the doors of the elevator opened she found herself standing in a desolate wasteland covered in garbage and filth. She saw her friends were dressed in rags and were picking up the garbage and putting it in sacks. The Devil came up to her and put his arm around her. "I don't understand," stammered the woman, "yesterday I was here and there was a golf course and a country club and we ate lobster and we danced and had a great time. Now all is a wasteland of garbage and all my friends look miserable."

The Devil looked at her and smiled. "Yesterday we were recruiting you; today you're staff."

FIVE RIVERS OF HELL/HADES

Name	Greek Root	Meaning
1. Acheron	*achos-reo*	grief-flowing
2. Cocytus	*kokuo*	to weep
3. Lethe	*letle*	oblivion
4. Phlegethon	*phleo*	to burn
5. Styx	*stugeo*	to loathe

SIN

The Seven Deadly (or Capital) Sins

Sin	Punishment in Hell	Color	Animal	Alternate Symbol
Pride	Broken on the wheel	Violet	Horse	Lion
Envy	Placed in freezing water	Green	Dog	Dog
Anger	Dismembered while alive	Red	Bear	Lion
Sloth	Thrown into snake pits	Light Blue	Goat	Ass
Greed	Placed into boiling oil	Yellow	Frog	Man at desk
Gluttony	Forced to eat vermin	Orange	Pig	Ram
Lust	Smothered in fire	Blue	Cow	Sow

See the Seven Heavenly Virtues, page 25

Helpful Hints Concerning
the Seven Deadly Sins

1. The seven deadly sins can be found within the Bible, but they were also enumerated by Pope Gregory the Great (604) in *Moralia in Job*.
2. Originally, "sloth" was sadness, or *tristia*, but it was later changed.
3. Previously, eight "principal" vices had been explicated by a writer named Cassian, in the fourth century.
4. These sins were called "capital" sins by the Church, as opposed to venial sins. Venial sins were those that could be forgiven, but the capital sins could have a permanent effect on one's fate and spiritual health and welfare.

Seven Different Ways (Graphic Schemes)
in Which the Seven Deadly Sins
Are Depicted or Illustrated

Tree • Wheel • Scenes • As Parts of a Naked Man
As Parts of a Woman • Around a Clothed Man
Animals

Seven Deadly Sins,
According to Gandhi

Wealth Without Work • Pleasure Without Conscience
Science Without Humanity • Knowledge Without Character
Politics Without Principle • Commerce Without Morality
Worship Without Sacrifice

Heaven and Hell
Ways to Cleanse Yourself of Sin

LENT: A holiday beginning forty days before Easter, in which those observing use fasting or abstinence from specific foods as a way to clear space for self-reflection. A time for prayer and penance.

YOM KIPPUR (working tag team–style with Rosh Hashanah): The Jewish Day of Atonement, this holiday concludes a period beginning with Rosh Hashanah, in which individuals seek forgiveness and "right" their "wrongs."

DASSEHRA: The last day of a ten-day festival that honors specific goddesses, this holiday is a celebration of the triumph of good over evil.

RAMADAN: In some ways similar to Yom Kippur, Ramadan is also a fasting holiday, though it lasts for a full month, in contrast to Yom Kippur's one day. During this holiday, one experiences poverty and deprivation; a solemn holiday.

CONFESSION: A Catholic sacrament of penance, in which the repentant confesses his or her sins and seeks forgiveness from a priest.

Sin,*
Defined by Various Religions

1. THOUGHTS: According to the Christian definition of sin, a thought can be sinful.
2. In JUDAISM, a thought is not sinful but can lead to sin.
3. LOST POTENTIAL/LAZINESS: According to Jewish tradition, a failure to live up to one's potential is a sin.
4. HAD IT FROM THE GET-GO: The idea of "original sin" is honored by Christian tradition (opposed by the Jewish religion), basically holding that we are "in sin" or "sinners" for the fact alone that we descended from Adam and Eve. In some millennial religious sects,

*The word "sin" was originally an archery term (*kheit*), which meant "to fall short of the mark." See "Lost Potential," above.

procreation is discouraged if not prohibited, with the idea that humans should not produce more humans until they are released from this original sin, during the next coming.

5. ACTIONS: Fairly universal among religions, violent acts that violate God's commandments or laws are sinful.

BABY NAME FINDER, PART II

Baalzebub	The devil	Biblical	Male
Chesed	As a devil	Biblical	Male
Desdemona	Misery, Unlucky	Greek	Female
Garm	Guards the Gates of Hell	Norse	Male
Melloney	"The Black One"	Latin	Female
Naraka	Hell	Hindu	Male

POESY PRIMER: HELL

1. Bell
2. Cell
3. Dwell
4. Shell
5. Smell
6. Farewell
7. Night bell
8. Lapel
9. Lymph cell
10. Michelle (Miguel)
11. Magic spell
12. Oyster shell
13. Peach bell
14. Misspell
15. Gas well
16. Hair gel
17. Morel

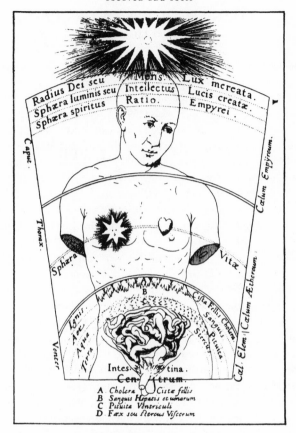

Relation of the Upper Heavens to Man
(*Ultriusque cosmi historia*) by Robert Fludd

According to Fludd's diagram, the seat of the soul is in the top of the skull (receiving increased light), the intellect is seated in the middle part, and the whole head is assigned to reason. The thorax correlates with heaven, and the orbit of the sun influences the heart. The bile and gallbladder are influenced by fire, air is the blood that runs through both the liver and veins, and water is the phlegm of the stomach. Waste through the intestines is earth.

SATANISM, OR DEVIL WORSHIP
A Brief History

It's unclear when, exactly, Satanism or devil worship truly gained popularity, since "Satanism" was a blanket term often applied to any perceived deviation from the religious norm at several points in history, including the Salem witchcraft trials (1692). Gnostics are often "blamed" for spreading devil worship. Though many early devil worshippers still considered Jesus Christ their savior (and the man to deliver them from an evil God), they considered earth itself to be hell, and humans to be a race of people created by rebel angels (Archons). This reversal, however (God is evil and Satan is good), is at the crux of the conflict between devil worshippers and mainstream Christianity. In the Middle Ages, several trials for satanic worship are documented but it's unclear to what extent the group's members identified themselves as devil worshippers. Cathars, who emerged in southern France, also in the Middle Ages, believed that God was evil. They adopted a dualist position, which delineated between the evil God and another rival, kind God. Cathars believed it was wrong to procreate (since this was the command of the evil God of the Old Testament), own property, or eat animals, among other things. In the thirteenth century, Luciferians appeared. They proposed that Lucifer had been unjustly cast from heaven and that, ultimately, Lucifer and his "sinful" sidekicks would return to heaven and overthrow God (a rumble in heaven, of sorts). Some people recognize the first roots of modern-day Satanism in the eighteenth century, during a period of Romanticism, when intellectualism flourished and works like *Paradise Lost* were published. Various thinkers along with several books cast Satan in a light other than that cast on him by Christianity. Satan was offered as a figure rebelling and fighting for freedom. Several small associations and societies came out of these ideas; the most famous example is the Hellfire Club of Great Britain. More recently, in 1966—the same year the Black Panthers were founded—the Church of Satan was established. Founded by Anton Szandor LaVey (1930–1997), the church's current high priestess is Peggy Nadramia. Three years after LaVey declared the church's existence, *The Satanic Bible* was published. The Swedish Satanist Church has issued a simplified definition of Satanism, which clarifies that Satan is looked at, in this faith, as a symbol of man's nature (as opposed to a fallen angel), an individual of freedom with an unrepressed dark side. Perhaps this clarification was necessary due to recent publicity concerning cultlike rituals involving human sacrifice. The media have largely overplayed these incidents though people claiming to worship Satan have certainly done some heinous things in his name. Still, these people may or may not be loosely affiliated with the Church of Satan, and may not understand its concepts. A note of interest: According to several rumors, Anton LaVey played Satan in Roman Polanski's *Rosemary's Baby* (1968).

See Paradise Lost, Rosemary's Baby

DO YOU KNOW THE BLUE DEVILS IN YOUR NEIGHBORHOOD?

1. CONCORD BLUE DEVILS: A drum corps founded in 1957 by Ann and Tony Odello. The Odellos named the corps after the VFW's color (blue) and Concord's local attraction Mount Diablo. In 1958, the corps added glockenspiels, changing from a strictly drum corps to a drum and bell corps, ultimately adding a bugle corps in 1970. Their success in competitions inspired a Blue Devils Music School, which teaches children, ages four and up. The Blue Devils have traveled to Japan, Korea, Italy, Australia, and the Netherlands, among other places, in competition.
2. THE FREDONIA STATE BLUE DEVILS: An ice hockey team based at Fredonia State University, Fredonia, New York. For recruitment information, go to: http://www.fredonia.edu/athletics/hockey/questionnaire.htm.
3. MOUNT MORRIS BLUE DEVILS: High schoolers from Mount Morris, New York.
4. DUKE BLUE DEVILS: Both the women's and men's teams are made of Blue Devils, named after "Les Diables Bleus," the well-known French soldiers who used their unique training to fight in the Alps. For the past four years, the female Blue Devils have been a

number-one seed in the NCAA tournament. The Associated Press poll has recently ranked the team in the country.

5. HAMBURG BLUE DEVILS: American Football in Hamburg. Football, literally, not soccer. German Bowl Champions in 1996, 2001, 2002, and 2003. Euro Bowl Champions in 1996, 1997, and 1998. Of the ninety-nine players, only six are American.

6. BLUE DEVILS OF CENTRAL CONNECTICUT STATE: College students of CCS.

7. LAKE FENTON BLUE DEVILS: High school students at Lake Fenton School, in Fenton, Michigan.

8. UW STOUT BLUE DEVILS: Athletes at the University of Wisconsin's Stout campus, in Menomonee, Wisconsin.

9. THE LAST OF THE BLUE DEVILS: The full title of the film is *The Last of the Blue Devils: The Kansas City Jazz Story*, and it chronicles the 1979 reunion of jazz greats including Count Basie, Jay McShann, and others. The Blue Devils were an early Kansas City jazz band.

10. KERI LEIGH AND THE BLUE DEVILS: Most recently recorded an album titled *Hell and Back*.

11. HURRICANE AND BLUE DEVILS: A Norwegian blues band playing in the style of Stevie Ray Vaughan and other American musicians.

See Blue Angels, page 58

ISLANDS OF THE BLEST
In Greek mythology, those residing on the White Island or the Islands of the Blest were considered immortal

"The Three-Decker" by Rudyard Kipling
"~The three-volume novel is extinct.~"

Full thirty foot she towered from waterline to rail.
It cost a watch to steer her, and a week to shorten sail;
But, spite all modern notions, I found her first and best—The only certain packet for the Islands of the Blest.

Heaven and Hell

Fair held the breeze behind us—'twas warm with lovers' prayers.
We'd stolen wills for ballast and a crew of missing heirs.
They shipped as Able Bastards till the Wicked Nurse confessed,
And they worked the old three-decker to the Islands of the Blest.

By ways no gaze could follow, a course unspoiled of Cook,
Per Fancy, fleetest in man, our titled berths we took
With maids of matchless beauty and parentage unguessed,
And a Church of England parson for the Islands of the Blest.

We asked no social questions—we pumped no hidden shame—
We never talked obstetrics when the Little Stranger came:
We left the Lord in Heaven, we left the fiends in Hell.
We weren't exactly Yussufs, but—Zuleika didn't tell.

No moral doubt assailed us, so when the port we neared,
The villain had his flogging at the gangway, and we cheered.
'Twas fiddle in the forc's'le—'twas garlands on the mast,
For every one got married, and I went ashore at last.

I left 'em all in couples a-kissing on the decks.
I left the lovers loving and the parents signing cheques.
In endless English comfort by county-folk caressed,
I left the old three-decker at the Islands of the Blest!

That route is barred to steamers: you'll never lift again
Our purple-painted headlands or the lordly keeps of Spain.
They're just beyond your skyline, howe'er so far you cruise
In a ram-you-damn-you liner with a brace of bucking screws.

Swing round your aching search-light—'twill show no haven's peace.
Ay, blow your shrieking sirens to the deaf, gray-bearded seas!
Boom out the dripping oil-bags to skin the deep's unrest—And you
aren't one knot the nearer to the Islands of the Blest!

Heaven and Hell

But when you're threshing, crippled, with broken bridge and rail,
At a drogue of dead convictions to hold you head to gale,
Calm as the Flying Dutchman, from truck to taffrail dressed,
You'll see the old three-decker for the Islands of the Blest.

You'll see her tiering canvas in sheeted silver spread;
You'll hear the long-drawn thunder 'neath her leaping figure-head;
While far, so far above you, her tall poop-lanterns shine
Unvexed by wind or weather like the candles round a shrine!

Hull down—hull down and under—she dwindles to a speck,
With noise of pleasant music and dancing on her deck.
All's well—all's well aboard her—she's left you far behind,
With a scent of old-world roses through the fog that ties you blind.

Her crew are babes or madmen? Her port is all to make?
You're manned by Truth and Science, and you steam for steaming's sake?
Well, tinker up your engines—you know your business best—
She's taking tired people to the Islands of the Blest

FEARS

1. Uranophobia, or Ouranophobia: A fear of heaven; not to be confused
   with Urophobia, fear of urinating.
2. Uranomania: The delusion that one is of divine descent.
3. Uranomancy: Divination through consultation with the heavens.
4. Stygiophobia, or Hadephobia: A fear of hell.
5. Satanophobia: Fear of the devil.
6. Thanatophobia: Fear of death or dying.

Other phobias related to heaven and hell:
Pitchforkphobia • Electrohalophobia • Acrophobia (heights)
Nephophobia (clouds)

ANGEL-BEAST:
A SEVENTEENTH-CENTURY
CARD GAME

(or La Bête)

NUMBER OF PLAYERS: 2 to 10
DATE REDACTED: October 30, 1995
REDACTOR: Rose Alessandro de Firenze
OTHER PLAYERS: Stefan Skywatcher, Marian of Edwinstowe

This game uses a standard French-suited 52-card deck.

Play

Before dealing, each player antes an agreed-upon number of cards (the same total for each player) into each of three piles: the "king of trump" pile, the "play" pile, and the "triolet" pile. Five cards are dealt to each player, starting to the dealer's left. The top card is turned over to determine trump and remains on the table during play. Play proceeds as in standard trick games, with kings high, aces low. At the end of each hand (when all the tricks have been taken), five cards are again dealt to each player, with the person who took the last trick in the previous hand leading the current one. Play continues until you can no longer deal a complete hand of five cards to each player. (Note: this will differ according to the number of players.) When you've run through the deck, check for victory conditions. The person with the most tricks wins the "play" pile; the person with the king of trump wins the "king of trump" pile; and the person with the highest triolet (three of a kind) wins the "triolet" pile. In the event that no one definitively wins a particular pile (e.g., two people tie for the highest number of tricks) that pile remains on the table through subsequent game(s) until someone does win it.

DANTE'S *INFERNO*: A PRIMER

Note: These nine circles of hell are taken from the *Inferno*, the first part of Dante Alighieri's *Divine Comedy* trilogy.

Ring	Topography	Beasts/Demons	Sin	Specific Souls
1. One: Limbo			Not Baptized	Poets of Antiquity
2. Two: Lust		Minos	Lust	Paolo and Francesca
3. Three: Gluttony		Cerberus	Gluttony	Ciacco
4. Four: Avarice		Plutus	Spending/Hoarding	
5. Five: Anger		Phlegyas	Wrath	Filippo Argenti
6. Six: Heresy		Furies	Heresy	Epicurus, Farinata
7. Seven: Violence	3 rings	Minotaur/Harpies	Violence Toward Another	Attila, Rinieri
			Suicide	Pier della Vigna
			Blasphemy	Capaneus
			Sodomy	Brunetto Latini
			Usury	Usurous families

8. Eight: Fraud	10 pouches	The Malebranche	Seducers	Caccianemico, Jason
			Flatterers	Alessio Interminei
			Simoniacs	Pope Nicholas III
			Diviners/Sorcerers	Manto, Michael Scott
			Barrators/Grafters	The Navarrese
			Hypocrites	The Jovial Friars
			Thieves	Vanni Fucci
			False Counselors	Ulysses
			Schismatics	Bertran de Born
			Falsifiers	Gianni Schicchi
9. Nine: Betrayal	1 pit of hell + 4 other realms	Giants/Lucifer	of Kin	Mordred
			of Country/Party	Ugolino
			of Guests	Friar Alberigo
			of Benefactors	Brutus, Judas

Limbo, from Gustave Doré's illustrations for Dante's *Divine Comedy*.

"BALLADE TO OUR LADY"

Written for his Mother

Dame du ciel, regents terrienne,
Emperiere des infemaux palus. . . .

Lady of Heaven and earth, and therewithal
Crowned Empress of the nether clefts of Hell,—

I, thy poor Christian, on thy name do call,
Commending me to thee, with thee to dwell,
Albeit in nought I be commendable.

Heaven and Hell

But all mine undeserving may not mar
Such mercies as thy sovereign mercies are;
Without the which (as true words testify)
No soul can reach thy Heaven so fair and far.
Even in this faith I choose to live and die.
Unto thy Son say thou that I am His,
And to me graceless make Him gracious.
Said Mary of Egypt lacked not of that bliss,
Nor yet the sorrowful clerk Theopbilus,
Whose bitter sins were set aside even thus
Though to the Fiend his bounden service was.
Oh help me, lest in vain for me should pass
(Sweet Virgin that shalt have no loss thereby!)
The blessed Host and sacring of the Mass
Even in this faith I choose to live and die.

A pitiful poor woman, shrunk and old,
I am, and nothing learn'd in letter-lore.
Within my parish-cloister I behold
A painted Heaven where harps and lutes adore,
And eke an Hell whose damned folk seethe full sore:
One bringeth fear, the other joy to me.
That joy, great Goddess, make thou mine to be,—
Thou of whom all must ask it even as I;
And that which faith desires, that let it see.
For in this faith I choose to live and die.

O excellent Virgin Princess! thou didst bear
King Jesus, the most excellent comforter,
Who even of this our weakness craved a share
And for our sake stooped to us from on high,
Offering to death His young life sweet and fair.
Such as He is, Our Lord, I Him declare,
And in this faith I choose to live and die.

—François Villon, from *Poems*, Dante Gabriel Rossetti, trans. (Boston: Roberts Brothers, 1870), pp. 178– 79.

DIVINATION

Robert Fludd's *Utriusque cosmi maioris*, 1617.
Courtesy of the Fortean Picture Library.

Condemned by the Hebrew Bible, divination has been practiced for hundreds and even thousand of years by those who wish to ascertain the will of God. Priests used to roll dice called the Urim and Thummin, while methods still used frequently today include reading tea leaves, astrology, and tarot card reading. Those religiously opposed to divination argue that diviners are keeping company with the devil.

Heaven and Hell

From the *Provincial Freeman*,
March 7, 1857, Chatham, Canada

RETORT COURTEOUS.—While two little girls, one the daughter of a clergyman and the other, the child of one of his parishoners were playing together; they fell into an angry dispute, as children often will in imitation of their seniors. To mortify and spite her antagonist, the layman's girl saw fit to remind her of her father's well known poverty, and intimated [to] her tartly, "that had it not been for her father's benevolent interference, the poor minister would have been in the work-house."

"Well, I don't care," replied the other, "if it had not been for my father, *yours* would have been in *hell* long ago!"

WHAT IS TO-MORROW

From the *Provincial Freeman*,
June 14, 1856, Chatham, Canada

I asked an aged man, a man of thought,
Who shook his [ ] curls, but answered not?
His mum was the . . . . gives
That none could solve the question under heaven.
. . . . With meditation, the sage thus replied;
Man hath scan'd the earth and sea, ere he died,
But none hath lived so long, or breath as yet
To see to-morrow's sun e'er rise or set.
I asked the King upon his azure throne,
Who rules supremely o'er the spangled dome,
And lends the starry [ ] their borrow'd light,
To deck and beautify the solemn night;
And he replied (no tongue could speak so wise)
To-morrow's vail'd when I illume the skies;
'Tis enough for thee to know, for thee to say,
When I appear, it is the present day:
I asked Urania with her golden lyre,
Who moved the gods with pure harmonic fire;

She said, what is to-morrow, dost thou ask,
I would like to answer, but ho! the task
To draw the curtain, or delineate,
The mistic scenery of a future state.
Methinks, 'tis a mite of dark duration,
Recon'd with time by imagination,
And like a pleasing phantom of the breast,
It bid the weak o seek for idle rest;
And crowd that hidden mite (through fond delay)
With the duties of this the present day.
I asked a soul—a soul forever lost,
It shriek'd, and tried to lisp the Saviours cross;
But a hollow murmur rose from the cell.
To-morrow it said, sank me down to hell.—
Go quickly—tell thy friends, thy neighbors all
To mark the present and obey the call;
Or like unto me, they'll weep with sorrow,
Ere they will see, the far distant 'morrow.

ANONYMOUS.
Dresden, June 5th.

UNE FÊTE: THE SAINTS AND SINNERS BALL

Billed as Australia's premier adult event, this ball is an erotic sexcapade of a party, bringing satisfactory sin to more than 21,500 people in the past ten years. Each ball has a specific theme, such as "Red Devils— Come dressed 'hot as hell,' and 'devilishly good.'" Amenities include private fun areas and the famous "Grope Box." The entertainment starts early with strippers and dirty dancing. In 2002, 750 people attended. Join the Sinners Club and receive the *Saints Newsletter*, which keeps members apprised of future events.

NORSE MYTHOLOGY AND ITS NINE WORLDS

Realm	World	Ruler / Resident
Upper	Asgard	Odin /Aesir
Upper	Vanaheim	/Vanir
Upper	Alfheim	Freyr /Elves
Below	Midgard ("Middle Earth")	/Humans
Below	Jotunheim	/Giants
Below	Svartalfheim	/Dark Elves
Land of the Dead	Niflheim	Goddess Hel/
Land of the Dead	Muspelheim	/Fire Giants
Land of the Dead	Hel	/dead people

The Upper realm and Below are connected by Bifrost, which is a rainbow bridge. Roughly, we can say that the Upper realms correspond to "heaven" or "heavens," plural, and that the Land of the Dead corresponds to various levels of hell.

Hel, goddess of the Netherworld

Hel: In Norse mythology or Asatru, Hel denotes both a person and a place. 1. As a person, Hel was the daughter of Loki. After she was exiled to the underworld by Odin, she became ruler there. 2. As a place, Hel denotes the underworld itself, a place of the dead, and one of the nine worlds that make up the cosmography of Norse mythology. The pronunciation is the same as that of "hell."

Other important figures:

ODIN: Odin, the father of the Norse gods, is akin to Zeus of Greek mythology. One-eyed, Odin is the father and head of all other Norse gods and goddesses, therefore ruling the nine worlds, which comprise those realms akin to heaven and hell. *See alternatives to heaven and hell, pages 1, 5.*

LOKI: A brother of Odin, and a powerful god himself, Loki is known as both a troublemaker and a problem solver.

Though ancient in origin, Norse mythology continues to constitute a faith of sorts, under the term Asatru, which bases itself not only on the stories of Norse gods and goddesses but also on the Nine Noble Virtues. Asatru experienced a resurgence of interest in the 1970s.

HOW TO DATE AN ASATRUER

1. Visit your closest Wiccan bookstore.
2. Search in the Grove directory, an online service featuring "kindred" groups all across the United States. You'll find groups such as Mjolnier's Lightning Kindred, of Idaho, and Wolfhammer Kindred, in Kansas.
3. Recently, a Web site sympathetic to the cause of single Asatruers was created. See the personals: http://huginn.ealdriht.org/personals.html. Please note the webmaster's warning: "While others are invited to use the personals, please do so only if you are willing to be in a relationship with someone following Germanic Heathenry."

HA-HA IN HEAVEN: JOKES
New Yorkers Arrived

One day at the entrance to heaven, St. Peter saw a New York street gang walk up to the Pearly Gates. This being a first, St. Peter ran to God and said, "God, there are some evil, thieving New Yorkers at the Pearly Gates. What do I do?"

God replied, "Just do what you normally do with that type. Redirect them down to hell."

St. Peter went back to carry out the order and all of a sudden he comes running back yelling, "God, God, they're gone, they're gone!"

"Who, the New Yorkers?"

"No, the Pearly Gates."

Making Comparisons

In Heaven:
1. The cooks are French
2. The policemen are English
3. The mechanics are German
4. The lovers are Italian
5. The bankers are Swiss

In Hell:
1. The cooks are English
2. The policemen are German
3. The mechanics are French
4. The lovers are Swiss
5. The bankers are Italian

In Computer Heaven:
1. The management is from Intel
2. The design and construction are done by Apple
3. The marketing is done by Microsoft
4. IBM provides the support
5. Gateway determines the pricing

Heaven and Hell

In Computer Hell:

1. The management is from Apple
2. Microsoft does design and construction
3. IBM handles the marketing
4. The support is from Gateway
5. Intel sets the price

Bring Riches with You

There once was a rich man who was near death. He was very grieved because he had worked hard for his money, and he wanted to be able to take it with him to heaven. So he began to pray that he might be able to take some of his wealth with him.

An angel hears his plea and appears to him. "Sorry, but you can't take your wealth with you." The man implores the angel to speak to God to see if He might bend the rules.

The man continues to pray that his wealth could follow him. The angel reappears and informs the man that God has decided to allow him to take one suitcase with him. Overjoyed, the man gathers his largest suitcase and fills it with pure gold bars and places it beside his bed.

Soon afterward the man dies and shows up at the Gates of Heaven to greet St. Peter. St. Peter seeing the suitcase says, "Hold on, you can't bring that in here!" But the man explains to St. Peter that he has permission and asks him to verify his story with the Lord. Sure enough, St. Peter checks and comes back saying, "You're right. You are allowed one carry-on bag, but I'm supposed to check its contents before letting it through."

St. Peter opens the suitcase to inspect the worldly items that the man found too precious to leave behind and exclaims, "You brought pavement?!!!"

Fulfilling their Requests

There were three men who died and before God would let them into heaven, he gave them a chance to come back as anything they wanted.

The first guy said, "I want to come back as myself, but a hundred times smarter." So God made him one hundred times smarter.

The second guy said, "I want to be better than that guy, make me a thousand times smarter." So God made him one thousand times smarter.

The last guy decided he would be the best. So he said, "God, make me better than both of them, make me a million times smarter."

So God made him a woman!

Filling in for St. Peter

A famous professor of surgery died and went to heaven. At the Pearly Gates he was asked by the gatekeeper: "Have you ever committed a sin you truly regret?"

"Yes," the professor answered. "When I was a young candidate at the hospital of St. Lucas, we played soccer against a team from the Community Hospital, and I scored a goal, which was offside. But the referee did not see it, and the goal won us the match. I regret that now."

"Well," said the gatekeeper. "That is a very minor sin. You may enter."

"Thank you very much, St. Peter," the professor answered.

"I am not St. Peter," said the gatekeeper. "He is having his lunch break. I am St. Lucas."

Heaven and Hell
Clinton Is in Heaven

President Clinton died and knocked at the Pearly Gates. "Who goes there?" inquired St. Peter.

"It's me, Bill Clinton."

"What bad things did you do on earth?"

Clinton thought a bit and answered, "Well, I smoked marijuana, but you shouldn't hold that against me because I didn't inhale. And I lied, but I didn't commit perjury."

After several moments of deliberation St. Peter replied, "Okay, here's the deal. We'll send you someplace where it is very hot, but we won't call it 'Hell.' You'll be there for an indefinite period of time, but we won't call it 'eternity.' And don't 'abandon all hope' upon entering, just don't hold your breath waiting for it to freeze over."

He's Going to Heaven

Father Murphy walks into a pub in Donegal and says to the first man he meets, "Do you want to go to heaven?"

The man said, "I do, Father."

The priest said, "Then stand over there against the wall."

Then the priest asked a second man, "Do you want to go to heaven?"

"Certainly, Father," was the man's reply.

"Then stand over there against the wall," said the priest.

Then Father Murphy walked up to O'Toole and said, "Do you want to go to heaven?"

O'Toole said, "No, I don't, Father."

The priest said, "I don't believe this. You mean to tell me that when you die you don't want to go to heaven?"

O'Toole said, "Oh, when I die, yes. I thought you were getting a group together to go right now."

Credit: www.aha!jokes.com

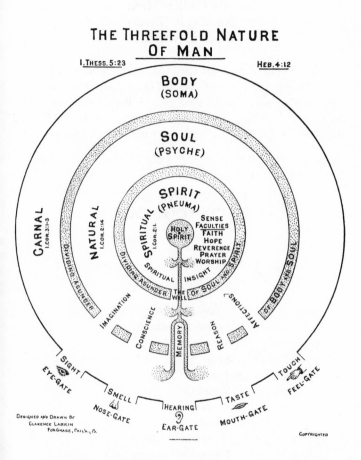

THE THREEFOLD NATURE OF MAN

In *The Threefold Nature of Man*, Clarence Larkin describes man as a "trinity" comprised of body, soul, and spirit; also known as *The Tabernacle of Man*. The courtyard represents his body, the "Holy Place" his soul, and the "Most Holy Place" his spirit.

A COOKBOOK:
Noshing in Nirvana,
Snacking with Satan

Yellow and White Angel Food Cake • Mock Angel Cake
Orange Angel Cake • Angel of Death Cheese Spread
Martha Washington Devil's Food Cake • Red Devil's Food Cake
Satanic (Deviled) Eggs • Mexican Deviled Eggs • Broiled Deviled
Tomatoes • Deviled Ham Puffs • Deviled Rock Lobster or Crab

YELLOW AND WHITE
ANGEL FOOD CAKE

Ingredients:
White part:
  6 egg whites
  ½ cup sugar
  ½ cup cake flour
  1 teaspoon cream of tartar
  Almond extract
  Salt
Yellow part:
  6 egg yolks
  ¾ cup sugar
  ¾ cup cake flour
  ¼ cup water, boiling
  1 teaspoon baking powder
  Vanilla
  Salt, a pinch

Directions for white portion: whip egg whites until frothy, add cream
of tartar and salt, whip until stiff. Fold in sugar and flour that has been
sifted together. Lastly, add almond extract.

Stir up the yellow part. Beat egg yolks and sugar together 3 minutes, add boiling water, vanilla, flour, baking powder, salt, sifted 3 times or more. Pour over white part and bake like an angel food cake.

Put in warm oven; increase temperature every 15 minutes. Bake about 60 minutes.

MOCK ANGEL CAKE

Ingredients:
- 1 cup sugar
- 1 cup flour
- 3 teaspoons baking powder
- ½ teaspoon salt
- 1 teaspoon vanilla
- 1 cup milk, scalded
- 2 egg whites

Directions: Sift dry ingredients together 4 times. Add milk slowly, stirring constantly. Lastly, add well-beaten egg whites. Bake in slow oven 50 minutes. Note: Slow oven is 300°–350°F.

ORANGE ANGEL CAKE

Ingredients:
- 1½ cups nonfat yogurt cheese
- 2 tablespoons orange juice concentrate
- 1 tablespoon honey
- 1 tablespoon grated orange rind

Heaven and Hell
Cake

¾ cups sifted unbleached flour
¼ cups sifted whole wheat pastry flour
12 egg whites, at room temperature
1½ teaspoons orange extract
1 teaspoon cream of tartar
½ cup honey
2 cups orange sections

Directions:

To make orange cream: In a medium bowl, fold together the yogurt cheese, orange juice concentrate, honey, and orange rind. Chill.

To make the cake: Sift the unbleached flour and pastry flour together. Return the flour to the sifter. In a 5- to 6-quart bowl, beat the egg whites with an electric mixer until bubbly. Add the orange extract and cream of tartar. Beat on medium speed until the whites form soft peaks. Gradually beat in the honey until the whites are stiff. Sift about ¼ cup of the flour over the whites. Carefully fold it in with a large spatula. Repeat until all the flour has been incorporated. Spoon batter into an ungreased 9-inch tube pan with removable bottom. Level top with a spatula. Bake at 325°F for about 40 to 50 minutes, or until the top is golden and springs back when lightly touched. Invert the pan onto a wire rack and let the cake cool for 1 hour. To remove the cake from the pan, run a thin knife around the outside edges. Remove the outer portion of the pan. Run a thin knife around the center tube and also around the bottom of the cake. Invert the cake onto a serving plate. Serve with the orange sections and orange cream. (If desired, place the cream in a pastry bag fitted with a star tip and pipe it decoratively around or onto each slice.)

NOTE: To make the yogurt cheese, spoon about 4 cups of nonfat yogurt into a sieve lined with a triple thickness of cheese cloth. Place over a bowl, cover and refrigerate for 4 hours, or until very thick.

ANGEL OF DEATH CHEESE SPREAD

Ingredients:
- 1 lb Gorganzola or Bleu cheese
- 1 lb ricotta cheese
- 2 cloves chopped garlic
- 1 cup chopped walnuts
- 4 fresh sage leaves
- Salt to taste
- Cheesecloth

Directions: Add garlic to ¼ cup of water in a small saucepan. Reduce to 2 tablespoons. Beat cheeses together. Add garlic mixture and salt, if desired. In a double layer of cheesecloth, put sage leaves in a pattern in the center. Sprinkle nuts on top. Put cheese mixture on top of nuts. Gather cheesecloth and form into a ball. Tie together. Put the cheese ball in a strainer over a dish and let sit in the fridge overnight to drain. Unwrap and serve!

MARTHA WASHINGTON DEVIL'S FOOD CAKE

Ingredients:
- 4 squares (1 oz) of unsweetened chocolate
- 2 cups sugar
- 1½ cups buttermilk
- 2 cups flour
- 1½ teaspoons baking powder
- 1 teaspoon baking soda
- 1 teaspoon salt
- ¾ cup butter or margarine
- 2 eggs
- 1 teaspoon vanilla

Directions: Melt chocolate in a saucepan over a very low heat, stirring constantly until smooth. Add ½ cup of the sugar and ½ cup of the buttermilk. Stir until well blended. Cool thoroughly. Mix flour, baking powder, soda, and salt. Cream butter and gradually beat in the remaining 1½ cups sugar. Continue beating until light and fluffy. Add eggs, one at a time, beating thoroughly after each. Blend in about one-fourth of the flour mixture, then add the chocolate and vanilla. Alternately, add the remaining flour and buttermilk, beating after each addition until smooth. Pour into two 9-inch greased and floured pans, and bake at 350°F for about 40 minutes. Use a cream cheese frosting on the outside and fill the space between the layers with a chocolate frosting.

RED DEVIL'S FOOD CAKE

Ingredients:
½ cup margarine
1½ cups sugar
2 eggs
1¾ cups flour
1¼ teaspoons baking soda
1 teaspoon salt
⅓ cup cocoa
1 cup milk
1 teaspoon vanilla

Directions: Cream margarine with sugar. Add eggs and beat till fluffy. Sift dry ingredients together and add alternately with milk and vanilla. Bake at 350°F in greased, 8 x 8-inch pan.

Serves 6

SATANIC (DEVILED) EGGS

Ingredients:
  3 large hard-cooked eggs
  2 tablespoons mayonnaise or salad dressing
  ½ teaspoon prepared mustard
  1 dash pepper

Directions: Cut eggs lengthwise into halves. Slip out yolks and mash with a fork. Mix in remaining ingredients. Fill the eggs with yolk mixture, heaping it up lightly.

MEXICAN DEVILED EGGS

Ingredients:
  12 hard-boiled eggs, large, peeled
  ¼ cup mayonnaise or salad dressing
  1 tablespoon cumin, ground
  1 tablespoon capers, finely chopped
  1 tablespoon mustard, prepared
  ½ teaspoon salt
  1 jalapeño pepper
  Red chiles, ground
  Cilantro, fresh, snipped

Directions: The jalapeño should be seeded and finely chopped. Cut the eggs lengthwise into halves. Slip out the yolks and mash with a fork. Mix the mashed yolks with the mayonnaise, cumin, capers, mustard, salt, and the jalapeño pepper. Fill the egg whites with the egg yolk mixture, heaping lightly. Sprinkle with ground red chiles and garnish with the cilantro.

Note: Though the precise origin of this moniker is not known, what we now know as "deviled eggs" were described as "stuffed eggs" as late as the fifteenth century, in an Italian cookbook, though they were called "deviled eggs" in a British cookbook by 1786.

BROILED DEVILED TOMATOES

Ingredients:
- 4 garlic cloves, mashed
- 1 tablespoon Dijon mustard
- ½ teaspoon dry mustard
- Salt and pepper to taste
- 2 tablespoons virgin olive oil
- 4 small tomatoes, halved

Directions: In bowl, combine garlic, Dijon mustard, and salt and pepper to taste. Add oil, drop by drop, whisking till smooth. Place tomatoes in buttered baking dish and spread with mustard mixture. Broil tomatoes 3 inches from heat for 1 minute or till tops are bubbly and golden.

DEVILED HAM PUFFS

Ingredients:
- 30 bread croutes, 5 cm
- Deviled ham paste
- 1 onion, finely chopped
- 2 teaspoons butter
- 125 grams cream cheese
- 1 cup grated cheese
- 1 egg yolk
- 2 teaspoons chives

Directions: 1. Spread each croute with ham paste. 2. Sauté onions in butter for 2 minutes. Allow to cool. 3. Beat the cream cheese until smooth; add next 3 ingredients and beat until well combined. Spread on top of ham paste. 4. Bake at 400°F for 10 minutes or until golden brown and heated. Serve immediately. To make croutes: 1. Cut bread circles from sliced bread with a 5 cm scone cutter. 2. Brush both sides of each croute with melted butter and place on scone tray. 3. Bake at 400°F for 10 minutes or until golden brown, turning during cooking time. Cool and store in an airtight container.

DEVILED ROCK LOBSTER OR CRAB

Ingredients:
¼ lb butter
1 medium onion, grated
2 teaspoons dried mustard
1 dash Tabasco sauce
Juice of 1 lemon
8 lobster tails or 1 lb lump crabmeat
4 tablespoons flour, heaping
2 cups milk
2 teaspoons salt
¼ cup sherry
2 tablespoons Parmesan cheese

Directions: This recipe is equally good with lump crabmeat or using the frozen lobster tails, whichever is available. Melt butter. Add onion that has been grated along with onion juice. Cook a few minutes until onion is tender. Add dried mustard, salt, then flour. Slowly add milk and make your cream sauce. Allow your sauce to thicken, stirring constantly, and then add all the other ingredients. Serve this in flaky pastry shells. This will serve six.

"GENERAL WILLIAM BOOTH ENTERS INTO HEAVEN" BY VACHEL LINDSAY

[To be sung to the tune of "The Blood of the Lamb"
with indicated instrument]

I

[Bass drum beaten loudly.]

Booth led boldly with his big bass drum—
(Are you washed in the blood of the Lamb?)
The Saints smiled gravely and they said: "He's come."
(Are you washed in the blood of the Lamb?)
Walking lepers followed, rank on rank,
Lurching bravoes from the ditches dank,
Drabs from the alleyways and drug fiends pale—
Minds still passion-ridden, soul-powers frail:—
Vermin-eaten saints with mouldy breath,
Unwashed legions with the ways of Death—
(Are you washed in the blood of the Lamb?)

[Banjos.]

Every slum had sent its half-a-score
The round world over. (Booth had groaned for more.
Every banner that the wide world flies
Bloomed with glory and transcendent dyes.
Big-voiced lasses made their banjos bang,
Tranced, fanatical they shrieked and sang:—
"Are you washed in the blood of the Lamb?"
Hallelujah! It was queer to see
Bull-necked convicts with that land make free.
Loons with trumpets blowed a blare, blare, blare
On, on upward thro' the golden air!
(Are you washed in the blood of the Lamb?)

Heaven and Hell

II

[Bass drum slower and softer.]

Booth died blind and still by Faith he trod,
Eyes still dazzled by the ways of God.
Booth led boldly, and he looked the chief
Eagle countenance in sharp relief,
Beard a-flying, air of high command
Unabated in that holy land.

[Sweet flute music.]

Jesus came from out the court-house door,
Stretched his hands above the passing poor.
Booth saw not, but led his queer ones there
Round and round the mighty court-house square.
Yet in an instant all that blear review
Marched on spotless, clad in raiment new.
The lame were straightened, withered limbs uncurled
And blind eyes opened on a new, sweet world.

[Bass drum louder.]

Drabs and vixens in a flash made whole!
Gone was the weasel-head, the snout, the jowl!
Sages and sibyls now, and athletes clean,
Rulers of empires, and of forests green!

*[Grand chorus of all instruments.
Tambourines to the foreground.]*

The hosts were sandalled, and their wings were fire!
(Are you washed in the blood of the Lamb?)
But their noise played havoc with the angel-choir.
(Are you washed in the blood of the Lamb?)
O, shout Salvation! It was good to see
Kings and Princes by the Lamb set free.
The banjos rattled and the tambourines
Jing-jing-jingled in the hands of Queens.

[*Reverently sung, no instruments.*]
And when Booth halted by the curb for prayer
He saw his Master thro' the flag-filled air.
Christ came gently with a robe and crown
For Booth the soldier, while the throng knelt down.
He saw King Jesus. They were face to face,
And he knelt a-weeping in that holy place.
Are you washed in the blood of the Lamb?

From *General William Booth Enters into Heaven and Other Poems*, published in 1913.

PROVERBS FROM PARADISE

1. In seventh heaven: joyful, ecstatic. According to early cosmography, the heavens were comprised of various levels. In early Jewish writings as well as Muslim scripture, the seventh heaven was the most elevated heaven. There, inhabitants were blissful.
2. Pennies from heaven: unexpected reward, especially monetary.
3. Stink to high heaven: smell terrible.
4. Move heaven and earth: triumph over obstacles, transcend what was previously considered impossible.
5. Heavens to Betsy: exclamation of surprise. People have argued about the expression's origins, tracing it back to Betsy Ross as well as to rifles that were called Old Betsys.
6. Heaven protects children, sailors, and drunken men: a self-explanatory proverb.
7. Fools rush in where angels fear to tread.

MEAT LOAF'S DISCOGRAPHY, AS IT RELATES TO HEAVEN AND HELL

1. BAT OUT OF HELL (1976): Described by one fan as a "Wagnerian Rock Opera," Meat Loaf's first album stayed on the UK charts for 400 weeks, the U.S. charts for 88 weeks, and remains one of

the top-selling albums in music history to date. Rereleased in 1991 and again in 2001.

2. HITS OUT OF HELL (1984): Released by CBS records.
3. ALIVE IN HELL (1987): Reissued in 1994.
4. HOT AS HELL (1992): One fan referred to this as "an Italian bootleg" (taken from a 1977 tour in Europe) though still worth the money for the unusual covers of "Johnny B. Goode" and "River Deep Mountain High."
5. HEAVEN AND HELL (1993): A compilation with Bonnie Tyler, this album features both Meat and Tyler on the cover as pleasingly plump heartthrobs.
6. BACK FROM HELL: THE VERY BEST OF MEAT LOAF: VOL. 1 (1993).
7. MEAT LOAF: LIVE OUT OF HELL (1993): Clearly a busy year for Meat Loaf or at least for the music packagers, who continued to recycle all of Meat Loaf's songs into new albums.
8. BAT OUT OF HELL II: BACK INTO HELL (1993): This album went platinum, and included a duet with Cher, "Anything for Love," which won a Grammy for Best Rock Vocal in 1994.
9. GET OUT OF HELL (1994): Mostly recorded at a concert in Cleveland in 1987, and later released in Germany in 1994 by Living Legend.
10. LOOK BACK INTO HELL (1994): An unofficial recording.
11. LIVE FROM HELL & MORE HELL HITS (Import), 2 CDs (1994): Released by BMG in Australia in 1994, with 15 studio tracks and 9 live tracks.
12. BACK FROM HELL AGAIN: THE VERY BEST OF MEAT LOAF: VOL. 2 (1994): A Sony release in Germany that included "A Time for Heroes," which was recorded for the Los Angeles Paralympic Games in 1987.
13. TO HELL AND BACK (1994): A 2-CD set released in Italy.
14. CHAT OUT OF HELL (Interview) (1994): Part of Baktabak's interview series with musicians and other artists.
15. HEAVEN CAN WAIT—THE BEST BALLADS OF MEAT LOAF VOL. 1 (1996): A Sony music album released in Germany.
16. LIVE BATS OUT OF HELL (1996): Another Italian bootleg.
17. FALLEN ANGEL (2003): A 2-CD compilation released by Sony.

Other related titles include: *Original Sin* (CD and LP), which includes the "Original Sin" CD single, performed with Taylor Dayne.

A MIX TAPE FOR YOUR SAINTLY FRIENDS AND FAMILY

Side I

"Undercover Agent," Alan O'Day
"Heaven's Just a Sin Away," The Kendalls
"Heaven's Beside You," Alice in Chains
"Hands to Heaven," Breathe
"Stairway to Heaven," Led Zeppelin
"Heaven," Bryan Adams
"Feels Like Heaven," Pete Cetera (with Chaka Khan)
"Heaven Is a Place on Earth," Belinda Carlisle
"Show Me Heaven," Maria McKee
"I Wish U Heaven," Prince
"Tears in Heaven," Eric Clapton
"Just Like Heaven," The Cure

Side II

"I Dreamed of a Hillbilly Heaven," Dolly Parton
"All You Want Is Heaven," Hall & Oates
"When I Get to Heaven," Ice Cube
"This Is Heaven to Me," Billie Holiday
"Doors of Heaven," Arlo Guthrie
"Heaven Can Wait," Iron Maiden
"Guitar Heaven," Neil Diamond
"Thank Heaven for Little Girls," Perry Como
"All That Heaven Will Allow," Bruce Springsteen
"Three Steps to Heaven," Sting
"It's a Long Way to Heaven," Partridge Family
"My Blue Heaven," Rudy Valee
"Little Trip to Heaven," Tom Waits

A HELLISH MIX TAPE:
BALLADS FOR BEELZEBUB

Side I

"Highway to Hell," AC/DC
"Disco Inferno," The Trammps
"Sympathy for the Devil," The Rolling Stones
"Sing You Sinners," Bing Crosby
"(You're the) Devil in Disguise," Elvis Presley
"Devil Inside," INXS
"Devil in Her Heart," Beatles
"Friend of the Devil," Grateful Dead
"Running With the Devil," Van Halen
"Devil Without a Cause," Kid Rock
"Hell to Pay," Bonnie Raitt
"Cigarettes in Hell," Oasis

Side II

"Hell Is for Children," Pat Benetar
"Hell's Bells," AC/DC
"If There's a Hell Below, We're All Going to Go," Curtis Mayfield
"Green Hell," Metallica
"Hell 4 a Hustler," Tupac Shakur
"Hell in Paradise," Yoko Ono
"Somewhere Between Heaven and Hell," Kiss
"Sam Hell," Helmet
"Heaven, Hell, or Houston," ZZ Top
"Run Like Hell," Pink Floyd
"Hell's Ditch," Pogues
"Hell Yeah," Ani DiFranco

SECOND-TO-HEAVEN HOLY SITES

1. HINDUISM: The Ganges River, especially the place where the Ganges meets other sacred rivers. The highest of these holy water spots is the intersection of the Ganges River with the Jamuna and the Sarasvati rivers. Followers of Hinduism equate the Ganges River with the goddess Ganga and believe she once flowed to heaven.
2. ISLAM: Muslims believe that Mecca, in Saudi Arabia, is the most sacred site on this planet, specifically recognizing it as the place where Adam and Eve reunited as well as the birthplace of Muhammad. Muslims pray in the direction of Mecca.
3. CATHOLICISM: The Vatican in Rome is actually considered an independent state, and was built in Rome because, historically, many Christians were persecuted in Rome, and also because St. Peter and St. Paul were crucified there.
4. MORMONISM: Salt Lake City was considered the New Zion when early church members first arrived there. Specifically the Salt Lake Temple on Temple Square is considered sacred ground for Mormons. Brigham Young himself laid the cornerstone of this temple in 1853. Only members can enter.
5. BAHA'I: Those of the Baha'i faith recognize two spots in Israel, Haifa and Acra, as holy sites. The Baha'i church maintains its world headquarters in Haifa.
6. JAINISM: This traditional Indian religion regards both the Shatrunjaya Hills of Gujrat and Mount Abu in Rajasthan as holy—both in India.
7. TAOISM: Mount Tai in China is a religious destination for Taoists, filled with religious temples and towers, among other Tao-related buildings.

GAMES THAT ARE SIMPLY DIVINE

1. HEAVEN AND HELL CHESS: In this variation of standard chess, the game is played on two stacked boards. The upper board represents heaven and the lower board represents hell. Pieces captured in heaven are sent to the lower board, or hell. Pieces captured in

hell are transferred back to heaven, where they are essentially "reincarnated."

2. HEAVEN QUEST: An animated Bible board game with four characters to choose from, including Knight, Spaceman, Baby, and Grandma. All players begin outside of Eden. Up to four players can play at one time.

3. ANGELS VS. DEVILS: In this PC game, the players pit heaven and hell against each other.

4. ARCHANGEL: This PC game follows in the sci-fi tradition, taking place in three different time periods.

5. DARK ANGEL: VAMPIRE APOCALYPSE: In this PlayStation 2 game, a deadly plague has attacked Anna's village, and her former friends and neighbors have transformed into flesh-eating monsters. The player of this game explores, as Anna, the cause of this epidemic.

6. SHADE: WRATH OF ANGELS: In this X-Box game, the player adopts the role of an ex-military mercenary, with options to morph into "the Demon" as necessary.

7. TITANIUM ANGELS: The protagonist of this PlayStation 2 game is a female warrior, fighting plasma weaponry and a host of bad guys.

8. ANGEL DEVOID: A first-person game set in a city obvious in likeness to New York. Unsurprisingly, this game involves a lot of shooting.

9. TECHNU: WRATH OF HEAVEN: A PlayStation 2 game boasting ninja action and adventure, along with "stealth attacks."

10. MIGHT AND MAGIC VI: THE MANDATE OF HEAVEN: This is a PC game in the tradition of role-playing games (not the kinky kind—think Dungeons and Dragons).

11. HEAVEN AND HELL: When playing this PC game, your agenda is to raise each village's level of belief in you through various prophets. Conversion is the name of the game. Your sustenance in this game is (what else, but) manna, which is used to cast spells and upgrade your housing situation. The main player, him- or herself, can choose to play on the good or evil side of things. Some players have complained that not enough distinction has been made between good and evil in this game. Perhaps this is what makes it so true-to-life.

12. HYBRID HEAVEN: Made for Nintendo, the premise of this game involves a U.S. space shuttle hijacking by an unknown species that now threatens the genetic makeup of the human race.

13. HELLBOY: Based on the popular comic, this PC game follows Hellboy and Sarah on their quest to save the world from evil. A film was released with the same name, also based on the comic, in 2004.

14. HELLFIRE: This PC game is an expansion of the original Diablo game, and is based on a simple plot. A demon named Na'Krul (a Diablo turncoat) is released from exile and establishes eight "levels" with names like the "Demon Crypt" and the "Festering Nest." Hellfire also adds to the stockpile of former weapons in Diablo I and Diablo II. Now, players have seven new spells and more than thirty new magical items, among other things.

15. ROAD TO INDIA: BETWEEN HELL AND NIRVANA: The story behind this PC game centers around Fred Reynolds, an American man who meets a beautiful Indian woman, named Anusha, at Yale University. Ultimately, Anusha is kidnapped and Fred travels to India to find her. As Fred, you'll explore India, though mainly you'll encounter only those elements of India that have already been overexoticized.

16. HELLBENDER: This PC game is plot-heavy. You're a solo pilot defending your galaxy. Those familiar with Microsoft's Fury 3 will recognize elements of Hellbender. Added bonus of this game: the voices of Russell Johnson (*Gilligan's Island*) and Gillian Anderson (*The X-Files*).

17. DEVIL MAY CRY: From PlayStation 2, this game follows a highly complex (or just confusing) plot wherein a swordsman named Spahda defeated a demon army by himself, purportedly 2,000 years ago, and now a private investigator (and son of Spahda) in an American city (named Dante, of course) wants to avenge the death of his mother and brother, using a sword no less. Leave common sense at home when playing this game.

18. DAREDEVIL: In this Game Boy game, players slog through the "underbelly of Hell's Kitchen" in New York City, working as the Daredevil to stomp out crime. Enemies encountered along the way include: Kingpin, Elektra, Bullseye, and the Sewer King. Anyone familiar with the gentrification of New York City's real-life Hell's Kitchen will be amused by this depiction.

19. DEVIL DICE: This PlayStation game begins where Tetris left off. Note that this new and improved version is many times more difficult in terms of challenge level.

PARADISE LOST:
A PRIMER WITH EXCERPTS

Gustave Doré's image from *Paradise Lost* (VI. 327, 328).
"Then Satan first knew pain,/And writhed him to and fro."

PARADISE LOST: An epic poem by John Milton, this gargantuan literary conquest was first conceived in 1639. It was initially printed in 1667 (in ten books) and again in 1674 (in twelve books). The theme of *Paradise Lost* is stated at the beginning, in Book I, as the Fall of Man through disobedience (i.e., eating the forbidden fruit, which is, in this story, not a proverbial victual). The poem is set first in Hell but later resituates itself in Heaven.

Heaven and Hell

Characters

Adam • Eve • God the Father • God the Son
Satan (Lucifer) • Angels • Demons

Summary

Book I: Satan and Beelzebub lie next to a burning lake, later scheming to build a palace to be called Pandemonium. By the end of Book I, it is built.

> Say first, for Heav'n hides nothing from thy view
> Nor the deep Tract of Hell, say first what cause
> Mov'd our Grand Parents in that happy State,
> Favour'd of Heav'n so highly, to fall off
> From their Creator, and transgress his Will
> For one restraint, Lords of the World besides?
> Who first seduc'd them to that fowl revolt?
> Th' infernal Serpent; he it was, whose guile
> Stird up with Envy and Revenge, deceiv'd
> The Mother of Mankinde, what time his Pride
> Had cast him out from Heav'n, with all his Host
> Of Rebel Angels, by whose aid aspiring
> To set himself in Glory above his Peers,
> He trusted to have equal'd the most High,
> If he oppos'd; and with ambitious aim
> Against the Throne and Monarchy of God
> Rais'd impious War in Heav'n and Battel proud
> With vain attempt. Him the Almighty Power
> Hurld headlong flaming from th' Ethereal Skie
> With hideous ruine and combustion down
> To bottomless perdition, there to dwell
> In Adamantine Chains and penal Fire,
> Who durst defie th' Omnipotent to Arms.

Book II: In this book, Satan debates hijacking heaven but opts instead to recover a third universe, other than Heaven and Hell, where he may exact his revenge. He travels through Hell, and through Hell's gates, which are unlocked by his offspring (Sin and Death).

> Thus SATAN; and him thus the Anarch old
> With faultring speech and visage incompos'd
> Answer'd. I know thee, stranger, who thou art,
> That mighty leading Angel, who of late
> Made head against Heav'ns King, though overthrown.
> I saw and heard, for such a numerous host
> Fled not in silence through the frighted deep
> With ruin upon ruin, rout on rout,
> Confusion worse confounded; and Heav'n Gates
> Pour'd out by millions her victorious Bands
> Pursuing. I upon my Frontieres here
> Keep residence; if all I can will serve,
> That little which is left so to defend
> Encroacht on still through our intestine broiles
> Weakning the Scepter of old Night: first Hell
> Your dungeon stretching far and wide beneath;
> Now lately Heaven and Earth, another World
> Hung ore my Realm, link'd in a golden Chain
> To that side Heav'n from whence your Legions fell:
> If that way be your walk, you have not farr;
> So much the neerer danger; goe and speed;
> Havock and spoil and ruin are my gain.

Book III: God learns of Satan's plan. Meanwhile, Satan describes himself as a cherub and fools the angel Uriel into showing him the way to earth.

Book IV: Satan ventures to the Garden of Eden, where he spies Adam and Eve, and experiences envy in response to their own bliss. The guardian angels find Satan here and throw him out of the garden. But not before he whispers into Eve's ear.

Heaven and Hell

While they adore me on the Throne of Hell,
With Diadem and Scepter high advanc'd
The lower still I fall, onely Supream
In miserie; such joy Ambition findes.
But say I could repent and could obtaine
By Act of Grace my former state; how soon
Would highth recal high thoughts, how soon unsay
What feign'd submission swore: ease would recant
Vows made in pain, as violent and void.
For never can true reconcilement grow
Where wounds of deadly hate have peirc'd so deep:
Which would but lead me to a worse relapse
And heavier fall: so should I purchase deare
Short intermission bought with double smart.
This knows my punisher; therefore as farr
From granting hee, as I from begging peace:
All hope excluded thus, behold in stead
Of us out-cast, exil'd, his new delight,
Mankind created, and for him this World.
So farwel Hope, and with Hope farwel Fear,
Farwel Remorse: all Good to me is lost;
Evil be thou my Good; by thee at least
Divided Empire with Heav'ns King I hold
By thee, and more then half perhaps will reigne;
As Man ere long, and this new World shall know.

Book V: Eve tells Adam of her terrible dream, and the angel Raphael
warns Adam of Satan's powers and his history.

Awake

My fairest, my espous'd, my latest found,
Heav'ns last best gift, my ever new delight,
Awake, the morning shines, and the fresh field
Calls us, we lose the prime, to mark how spring
Our tended Plants, how blows the Citron Grove,
What drops the Myrrhe, & what the balmie Reed,

135

How Nature paints her colours, how the Bee
Sits on the Bloom extracting liquid sweet.

Such whispering wak'd her, but with startl'd eye
On ADAM, whom imbracing, thus she spake.

O Sole in whom my thoughts find all repose,
My Glorie, my Perfection, glad I see
Thy face, and Morn return'd, for I this Night,
Such night till this I never pass'd, have dream'd,
If dream'd, not as I oft am wont, of thee,
Works of day pass't, or morrows next designe,
But of offence and trouble, which my mind
Knew never till this irksom night; methought
Close at mine ear one call'd me forth to walk
With gentle voice, I thought it thine; it said,
Why sleepst thou EVE? now is the pleasant time,
The cool, the silent, save where silence yields
To the night-warbling Bird, that now awake
Tunes sweetest his love-labor'd song; now reignes
Full Orb'd the Moon, and with more pleasing light
Shadowie sets off the face of things; in vain,
If none regard; Heav'n wakes with all his eyes,
Whom to behold but thee, Natures desire,
In whose sight all things joy, with ravishment
Attracted by thy beauty still to gaze.

Book VI: Raphael continues his story of Satan's fall, specifically recounting the rumble between Michael's army of angels and Satan and his army. Ultimately, Michael's angels pull up a mountain and throw it at Satan's ranks, but on the third day God sends his son in a flaming chariot to end the war. Satan and his ranks are pushed out of Heaven and into Hell.

So said, he o're his Scepter bowing, rose
From the right hand of Glorie where he sate,

And the third sacred Morn began to shine
Dawning through Heav'n: forth rush'd with whirlwind sound
The Chariot of Paternal Deitie,
Flashing thick flames, Wheele within Wheele undrawn,
It self instinct with Spirit, but convoyd
By four Cherubic shapes, four Faces each
Had wondrous, as with Starrs thir bodies all
And Wings were set with Eyes, with Eyes the Wheels
Of Beril, and careering Fires between;
Over thir heads a chrystal Firmament,
Whereon a Saphir Throne, inlaid with pure
Amber, and colours of the showrie Arch.
Hee in Celestial Panoplie all armd
Of radiant URIM, work divinely wrought,
Ascended, at his right hand Victorie
Sate Eagle-wing'd, beside him hung his Bow
And Quiver with three-bolted Thunder stor'd,
And from about him fierce Effusion rowld
Of smoak and bickering flame, and sparkles dire;
Attended with ten thousand thousand Saints,
He onward came, farr off his coming shon,
And twentie thousand (I thir number heard)
Chariots of God, half on each hand were seen.

Book VII: Raphael tells the story of God's decision to create a new world
with new beings to fill the void created by the fallen angels. Raphael
then describes the six days of creation.

. . . Whence ADAM soon repeal'd
The doubts that in his heart arose: and now
Led on, yet sinless, with desire to know
What neerer might concern him, how this World
Of Heav'n and Earth conspicuous first began,
When, and whereof created, for what cause,
What within EDEN or without was done
Before his memorie, as one whose drouth

Yet scarce allay'd still eyes the current streame,
Whose liquid murmur heard new thirst excites,
Proceeded thus to ask his Heav'nly Guest.

Book VIII: Adam wants to spend more time with Raphael and delays the angels' departure by telling Raphael his memory and experience of his own creation. When Raphael does finally depart, he leaves Adam with a reminder to beware of Satan's tricks.

take heed lest Passion sway
Thy Judgment to do aught, which else free Will
Would not admit; thine and of all thy Sons
The weal or woe in thee is plac't; beware.

Book IX: Satan enters the form of a serpent and approaches Eve when she's alone in the garden. She succumbs to the apple in the tree (the Tree of Knowledge), and then admits her deed to Adam, who decides to join her fate by eating of the fruit himself. Once they eat the apple and lose their innocence, they cover their bodies with leaves out of shame and self-consciousness. They awaken after a nap and accuse each other of bringing about this loss of innocence.

But confidence then bore thee on, secure
Either to meet no danger, or to finde
Matter of glorious trial; and perhaps
I also err'd in overmuch admiring
What seemd in thee so perfet, that I thought
No evil durst attempt thee, but I rue
That errour now, which is become my crime,
And thou th' accuser. Thus it shall befall
Him who to worth in Women overtrusting
Lets her Will rule; restraint she will not brook,
And left to her self, if evil thence ensue,
Shee first his weak indulgence will accuse.
Thus they in mutual accusation spent
The fruitless hours, but neither self-condemning,
And of thir vain contest appeer'd no end.

Book X: Satan returns to Hell and his palace, Pandemonium, victorious. His offspring (whom we met earlier at Hell's gates) are sent to earth. The son of God is sent to earth to judge Adam and Eve. Out of pity, he gives both of them clothes and waits several days for them to seek favor again with God. Satan and all of his angels are turned into serpents as punishment and they are reduced to hissing noises as an expression of victory.

Eve is despondent and proposes suicide but Adam reminds her that her "seed" will seek to avenge their plight. Adam also reminds her that their duty now is to reinstate their relationship with God.

> Th' other way *Satan* went down
> The Causey to Hell Gate; on either side
> Disparted *Chaos* over built exclaimd,
> And with rebounding surge the barrs assaild,
> That scorn'd his indignation: through the Gate,
> Wide open and unguarded, *Satan* pass'd,
> And all about found desolate; for those
> Appointed to sit there, had left thir charge,
> Flown to the upper World; the rest were all
> Farr to the inland retir'd, about the walls
> Of *Pandæmonium*, Citie and proud seate
> Of *Lucifer*, so by allusion calld,
> Of that bright Starr to *Satan* paragond.

Book XI: The couple is expelled from the garden but not before they've learned of events to come, including the great flood and the later covenant. These events along with other human plights to come, angel Michael explains, are the results of their transgression.

> So willingly doth God remit his Ire,
> Though late repenting him of Man deprav'd,
> Griev'd at his heart, when looking down he saw
> The whole Earth fill'd with violence, and all flesh
> Corrupting each thir way; yet those remoov'd,
> Such grace shall one just Man find in his sight,

That he relents, not to blot out mankind,
And makes a Covenant never to destroy
The Earth again by flood, nor let the Sea
Surpass his bounds, nor Rain to drown the World
With Man therein or Beast; but when he brings
Over the Earth a Cloud, will therein set
His triple-colour'd Bow, whereon to look
And call to mind his Cov'nant: Day and Night,
Seed time and Harvest, Heat and hoary Frost
Shall hold thir course, till fire purge all things new,
Both Heav'n and Earth, wherein the just shall dwell.

Book XII: Michael reveals the prophecy of the Messiah, and Adam is relieved that good will eventually come from his sin. Adam and Eve are led out of the garden of paradise and a flaming sword locks the gates of the garden so they cannot reenter.

In either hand the hastning Angel caught
Our lingring Parents, and to th' Eastern Gate
Led them direct, and down the Cliff as fast
To the subjected Plaine; then disappeer'd.
They looking back, all th' Eastern side beheld
Of Paradise, so late thir happie seat,
Wav'd over by that flaming Brand, the Gate
With dreadful Faces throng'd and fierie Armes:
Som natural tears they drop'd, but wip'd them soon;
The World was all before them, where to choose
Thir place of rest, and Providence thir guide:
They hand in hand with wandring steps and slow,
Through *Eden* took thir solitarie way.

Keep up with the latest in Paradise: check out *Paradise Regained* (1671), Milton's sequel to his first masterpiece.

OTHER BOOKS ON HEAVEN AND HELL

The Egyptian Heaven and Hell, E. A. Wallis Budge, 1899.

Heaven and Its Wonders and Hell: From Things Heard and Seen, Emanuel
Swedenborg. This book was first published in Latin in 1758. According to the Swedenborg Foundation's own abstract the book offers
"a detailed description of the afterlife into which people awaken after
the death of the physical body; about God, heaven, hell, angels, spirits, and devils . . . Somebody did come back to tell us about it, because God doesn't want to keep you in the dark."

The Doors of Perception and *Heaven and Hell*, Aldous Huxley, 1954, 1956.
Both Huxley works drive the same point home: Drugs offer new
spiritual insight and the opportunity to visit "other worlds." *Heaven
and Hell* specifically argues that hallucinogenics (mescaline, in particular) can provoke religious insight.

The Marriage of Heaven and Hell, William Blake, 1790. *See excerpt, page 154*

A Divine Revelation of Hell, Mary K. Baxter, Mark Baxter, and T. L.
Lowery, 1993

Between Heaven and Hell, Peter Kreeft, 1982. This book includes a dia-
logue between C. S. Lewis, Aldous Huxley, and John F. Kennedy,
about the afterlife.

One Minute After You Die: A Preview of Your Destination, Erwin W. Lutzer,
1997. This book is one of many that deserves a You've-Got-
Chutzpah Award for aiming to tell readers what happens after
death.

The Great Divorce, C. S. Lewis, 1945. This book follows protagonist
George MacDonald, who faces a dilemma when riding from hell
to heaven on a bus. Many passengers choose hell. What will Mr.
MacDonald choose and why?

Angels and Demons, Dan Brown, 2001.

The Five People You Meet in Heaven, Mitch Albom, 2003.

The Antichrist 666, William Josiah Sutton, 1995. This book aims to
answer the question: Who is the beast, identified with number
666?

Bringing Heaven into Hell, Merlin R. Carothers, 1984. In a nutshell: "Give praise to God though the earth is riddled with evil."

Hell Plus How to Avoid Hell, F. X. Schouppe, S. J., and Thomas A. Nelson, 1989. According to the discount Catholic Store's description, this book covers "mortal sins, Catholic attitude, marriage, divorce, purity, etc."

Books on Purgatory

Charity for the Suffering Souls, John A. Nageleisen, 1985. A how-to for those inclined to help "poor souls," as well as a description of the specific logistics involved in a purgatory stay, such as duration and extent of torment. Be warned!

Purgatory, Frederick Faber, 1950. This book describes the Catholic conception of purgatory.

HOW TO MAKE A SNOW ANGEL

Approach an abundantly snowy area, preferrably flat terrain. Lie down carefully with your back in the snow, arms and legs splayed from your torso. Slide arms and legs through snow, in an up-and-down motion, bringing your legs together and arms at your side, then all four limbs once again. Repeat until you've "carved" a path with your arms and legs. Carefully stand and look at your imprint, your "snow angel."

ANGELIC AND ARCHFIENDISH ART

1. ANGELS ON HORSEBACK, French School, twelfth century. Cathedral of St. Etienne, Auxerre, Burgundy, France.

2. ANNUNCIATORY ANGEL, Guido di Pietro Angelico, Italian, 1450–55. Detroit Institute of the Arts.

3. ARCHANGEL MICHAEL, Guariento di Arpo, Italian, fourteenth century. Museo Bottacin e Museo Civico, Padua.

4. CHILD ANGEL PLAYING A FLUTE, Bernadino Luini, Italian, 1500. Fitzwilliam Museum, University of Cambridge, UK.

5. CHRIST IN HELL, Friedrich Pacher, Austrian, 1460s. Museum of Fine Arts, Budapest.

6. DETAIL of two angels from Palazzo del Gran Consiglio, Baccio della Porta Bartolommeo, Italian, sixteenth century. Museo di San Marco dell'Angelico, Florence.

7. DEVILS, Frans Floris, Netherlandish, sixteenth century. Rafael Valls Gallery, London.

8. EARTHLY PARADISE, Flemish School, fifteenth century. Bibliotheque Royale de Belgique, Brussels.

9. FALL OF THE STAR OF SATAN, French School, thirteenth century. Bibliotheque Municipale, Cambrai, France.

10. FIGURES FOR A HEAVENLY LANDSCAPE, Bernadino India, Italian, sixteenth century. Hamburg Kunsthalle, Hamburg, Germany.

11. FIVE ANGELS DANCING BEFORE THE SUN, Giovanni di Paolo di Grazia, Italian, fifteenth century. Musée Conde, Chantilly, France.

12. GARDEN OF PARADISE, Master of Oberrheinischer, German, 1415. Stadelsches Kunstinstitut Frankfurt am Main, Germany.

13. GLIMPSE OF HELL, Flemish School, fifteenth century. Museo Correr, Venice.

14. GOOD AND EVIL ANGELS STRUGGLING FOR THE POSSESSION OF A CHILD, William Blake, English, c. 1795. Cecil Higgins Art Gallery, Bedford, Bedfordshire, UK.

15. GUARDIAN ANGEL, Andrea Pozzo, Italian, seventeenth century. Musée des Beaux-Arts, Caen, France.

16. HEAD OF AN ANGEL, Vincent van Gogh, after Rembrandt, Dutch, 1889. Private Collection.

17. HEAD OF AN ANGEL, Federico Fiori Baroccio, Italian, sixteenth century. Palazzo Pitti, Florence.

18. HEAD OF AN ANGEL, Italian School, fifteenth century. Private Collection.

19. HEAVEN AND HELL, Julio de Mantua, Italian, sixteenth century. Private Collection.

20. HEAVEN OPENED, George Jones, English, nineteenth century. Birmingham Museums and Art Gallery.

21. HELL, Dirck Bouts, Dutch, fifteenth century. Musée des Beaux-Arts, Lille, France.

22. HELL, Francois de Nome, French, seventeenth century. Musée des Beaux-Arts, Besancon, France.

23. IMPERIAL WORSHIP OF SHANGTI ON THE ALTAR OF HEAVEN AT PEKING, English School, 1883. Private Collection.

24. MARY—QUEEN OF HEAVEN, Master of the St. Lucy Legend, Italian, fifteenth century. Kress Collection, Washington, D.C.

25. MONUMENT TO THE ANGEL OF DEATH, Giovanni Lorenzo Bernini, Italian, seventeenth century, Duomo, Faenza, Italy.

26. PURGATORY, from *The Divine Comedy* by Dante Alighieri, Sandro Botticelli, Italian, 1480. Bibliotheque Nationale, Paris.

27. PURGATORY, from the *Psalterium Liturgicum*, French School, thirteenth century. Musée Conde, Chantilly, France.

28. SATAN AND BEELZEBUB, Gustave Doré, French, 1868. Private Collection.

29. SATAN PRESIDING AT THE INFERNAL COUNCIL, John Martin, English, nineteenth century. Victoria and Albert Museum, London.

30. SATAN, Henry Fuseli, Swiss, eighteenth century. Ashmolean Museum, University of Oxford, UK.

31. ST. JOHN NEPOMUK BEING TAKEN UP TO HEAVEN, Franz Anton Maulbertsch, German, eighteenth century. Private Collection.

32. TABLETOP OF THE SEVEN DEADLY SINS AND THE FOUR LAST THINGS, Hieronymus Bosch, Netherlandish, fifteenth century. Prado, Madrid.

33. THE ANGEL WITH AN OPEN BOOK, from *The Apocalypse of Angers*, Nicolas Bataille, French, 1373–87. Musée des Tapisseries. Also,

The Apocalypse of Angers contains scenes such as *The River of Paradise, The Second Angel Announces the Fall of Babylon,* and *The Fifth Trumpet and the Locusts.*

34. THE CELESTIAL ARMY, Ridolfo di Arpo Guariento, Italian, fourteenth century. Museo Civco, Padua, Italy.

35. THE DAMNED TORTURED ON THE WHEEL, from the Cycle of the Punishment of the Damned, Italian School, 1483. Sanctuary of Nostra Signora delle Grazie, Montegrazie, Italy.

36. THE DOORS OF HELL, Sir Edward Burne-Jones, English, nineteenth century. Private Collection.

37. THE FALL OF THE DAMNED, Frans II Francken, Flemish, seventeenth century. Kunsthistorisches Museum, Vienna.

38. THE FALL OF THE REBEL ANGELS, Pieter Brueghel, Netherlandish, 1562. Musée Royaux des Beaux-Arts de Belgique, Brussels.

39. THE GUARDIAN ANGEL WITH A GARLAND, Charles Filiger, French, 1892. Private Collection.

39. THE INFERNO, Henri met de Bles, Netherlandish, sixteenth century. Palazzo Ducale, Venice.

40. THE KINGDOM OF HEAVEN SUFFERETH VIOLENCE, Evelyn De Morgan, English, c. 1910. The De Morgan Centre, London.

41. THE LAST JUDGMENT, by Guido di Pietro Angelico, Italian, 1431. Museo di San Marco dell'Angelico, Florence.

42. THE LAST JUDGMENT, Hieronymus Bosch, Netherlandish, sixteenth century. Akademie der Bildenden Kunste, Vienna.

43. THE NARROW GATE TO HEAVEN AND THE WIDE GATE TO HELL, Cornelis de Bie, Dutch, seventeenth century. Johnny van Haeften Gallery, London.

44. THE NUPITAL BOWER WITH THE EVIL-ONE PEEPING AT THE CHARMS OF EDEN, James Gilray, English, 1797. Courtesy of the Warden and Scholard of New College, Oxford.

45. THE RESURRECTION OF THE DEAD FROM A GOSPEL, from Crimea, Armenian School, seventeenth century. Musée Conde, Chantilly.

46. THE TRIUMPH OF DEATH (detail of the damned in the pit of hell), Andrea di Cone Orcagna, Italian, 1348. Santa Croce, Florence.

47. THE TRIUMPH OF DEATH, Antoine Caron, French, sixteenth century. Musée d'Histoire de la Medecine, Paris.
48. THE VOICE OF THE DEVIL, William Blake, English, 1790–93. From *The Marriage of Heaven and Hell*, Fitzwilliam Museum, University of Cambridge, UK.
49. THREE ANGELS, Ridolfo Ghirlandaio, Italian, sixteenth century. Galleria dell'Accademia, Florence.

QUOTATIONS: HEAVEN

"The mind is its own place, and in itself/Can make a heaven of hell, a hell of heaven."

—John Milton, *Paradise Lost*, Book 1, I. 254, 1667

"Heaven sends us good meat, but the Devil sends cooks."

—David Garrick, "On Doctor Goldsmith's Characteristical Cookery," 1777

"Is it any better in Heaven, my friend Ford/Than you found it in Provence?"

—William Carlos Williams, "To Ford Madox Ford in Heaven," 1944

"A robin red breast in a cage/Puts all Heaven in a rage."

—William Blake, "Auguries of Innocence," 1803

"When the stars threw down their spears/And watered heaven with their tears:/Did he smile his work to see?/Did he who made the Lamb make thee?"

—William Blake, "The Tiger," *Songs of Experience*, 1794

"Parting is all we know of heaven,/And all we need of hell."

—Emily Dickinson, "My life closed twice before its close," published in 1896

"And she for him had given/Her all on earth, and more than all in heaven!"

—Thomas More, *The Corsair*, canto 3, st. 17, 1814

Heaven and Hell

"Give to me the life I love,/Let the lave go by me,/Give the jolly heaven
above/And the byway nigh me."

—Robert Louis Stevenson, "The Vagabond," *Songs of Travel*, 1895

"Two things fill the mind with ever new and increasing wonder and awe,
the more often and the more seriously reflection concentrates upon
them: the starry heaven above me and the moral law within me."

—Immanuel Kant, *Critique of Practical Reason*, 1788

"Bliss was it in that dawn to be alive,/But to be young was very heaven!"

—William Wordsworth, "The French Revolution,
as it Appeared to Enthusiasts," 1809

"I am not yet so lost in lexicography as to forget that words are the
daughters of earth, and that things are the sons of heaven. Language is
only the instrument of science, and words are but the signs of ideas: I
wish, however, that the instrument of the might be less apt to decay,
and that signs might be permanent, like the things which they denote."

—Samuel Johnson, preface to
A Dictionary of English Language, 1755

"God owns heaven/but He craves the earth."

—Anne Sexton, "The Earth," 1975

"In old days there were angels who came and took men by the hand
and led them away from the city of destruction. We see no white-winged
angels now. But yet men are led away from threatening destruction: a
hand is put into theirs, which leads them forth gently towards a calm
and bright land, so that they look no more backward; and the hand may
be a little child's."

—George Eliot, *Silas Marner*, 1861

"Heaven from all creatures hides the book of Fate,
All but the page prescrib'd, their present state."

—Alexander Pope, *Essay on Man*, 1734

Heaven and Hell

"A heaven so clear, an earth so calm,
So sweet, so soft, so hushed an air;
And, deepening still the dreamlike charm,
Wild moor-sheep feeding everywhere."

—Emily Brontë, "A Little While," 1838

"Heaven gives its favourites—early death."

—Lord Byron, *Childe Harold's Pilgrimage*, 1818

"For men at most differ as heaven and earth,/But women, worst and best, as heaven and hell."

—Alfred Tennyson, *Idylls of the King: Merlin and Vivien*, 1872

"Her angels face,
As the great eye of heaven, shyned bright,
And made a sunshine in the shady place."

—Edmund Spenser, *Faerie Queene, Book I*, 1590

"Every man is as Heaven made him, and sometimes a great deal worse."

—Miguel de Cervantes Saavedra, *Don Quixote*,
part ii, chapter iv, 1605

"Better to reign in hell, than serve in heaven."

—John Milton, *Paradise Lost*, Book 1, I. 263, 1667

"The blessed damozel leaned out
From the gold bar of Heaven:
Her eyes were deeper than the depth
Of waters stilled at even;
She had three lilies in her hand,
And the stars in her hair were seven."

—Dante Gabriel Rossetti, "The Blessed Damozel," 1847

Heaven and Hell

"Forth from his dark and lonely hiding-place
(Portentous sight!) the owlet Atheism,
Sailing on obscene wings athwart the noon,
Drops his blue-fring'd lids, and holds them close,
And hooting at the glorious sun in heaven
Cries out, 'Where is it?'"

—Samuel Taylor Coleridge, "Fears in Solitude," 1798

"Heaven is the work of the best and kindest men and women. Hell is the work of prigs, pedants and professional truth-tellers. The world is an attempt to make the best of Heaven and Hell."

—Samuel Butler, *Samuel Butler's Notebooks,* 1912

"Heaven must be an awfully dull place if the poor in spirit live there."
—Emma Goldman, *Red Emma Speaks,* part 2, published in 1972

"Heaven gives its glimpses only to those
Not in position to look too close."

—Robert Frost, "A Passing Glimpse," 1928

"Heaven is dumb, echoing only the dumb."
—Franz Kafka, *Dearest Father: Stories and
Other Writings,* published in 1954

"Heaven and hell suppose two distinct species of men, the good and the bad. But the greatest part of mankind float betwixt vice and virtue."
—David Hume, *Essays Moral, Political,
and Literary,* published in 1987

"Heaven is not one of your fertile Ohio bottoms, you may depend on it."
—Henry David Thoreau, letter, September 2, 1856,
to Daniel Ricketson

"Yes, Heaven is thine; but this
Is a world of sweets and sours;
Our flowers are merely—flowers,
And the shadow of thy perfect bliss
Is the sunshine of ours."

—Edgar Allan Poe, "Israfel," 1831

"To me heaven would be a big bull ring with me holding two barrera seats and a trout stream outside that no one else was allowed to fish in and two lovely houses in the town; one where I would have my wife and children and be monogamous and love them truly and well and the other where I would have my nine beautiful mistresses on nine different floors."

—Ernest Hemingway, letter, July 1, 1925, to F. Scott Fitzgerald

QUOTATIONS: HELL

"Hell is yourself [and the only redemption is] when a person puts himself aside to feel deeply for another person."

—Tennessee Williams, recalled on his death, 1983

"Hell hath no fury like a hustler with a literary agent."

—Frank Sinatra, quoted in December 1985

"Hell is other people."

—Jean-Paul Sartre, *No Exit*, 1947

"If there is a special Hell for writers it would be in the forced contemplation of their own works."

—John Dos Passos, *New York Times*, October 1959

"Yes, hell exists. It is not a fairy tale. One indeed burns there. This hell is not at the end of life. It is here. At the beginning. Hell is what the infant must experience before he gets to us."

—Dr. Frederick Leboyer, *New York Times*, December 1974

"A diplomat is a person who can tell you to go to hell in such a way that you actually look forward to the trip."

—Caskie Stinnett, *Out of the Red*, 1960

"An actor is ... at his best a kind of unfrocked priest who, for an hour or two, can call on heaven and hell to mesmerize a group of innocents."

—Alec Guinness, *Blessings in Disguise*, 1986

Heaven and Hell

"There is not a fiercer hell than the failure in a great object."
> —John Keats, preface to *Endymion*, 1818

"Let none admire
That riches grow in hell: that soil may best
Deserve the precious bane."
> —John Milton, *Paradise Lost*, Book I, 1667

"I follow up the quest
Despite of Day and Night and Death and Hell."
> —Alfred Tennyson, *Idylls of the King: Gareth and Lynette*, 1872

"A lifetime of happiness! No man alive could bear it: it would be hell on earth."
> —George Bernard Shaw, *Man and Superman*, 1905

"Hell is oneself,
Hell is alone, the other figures in it
Merely projections. There is nothing to escape from
And nothing to escape to. One is always alone."
> —T. S. Eliot, *The Cocktail Party*, Act 1, sc. 3, 1950

"Hell isn't merely paved with good intentions; it's walled and roofed with them. Yes, and furnished too."
> —Aldous Huxley, *Time Must Have a Stop*, 1944

"A belief in hell and the knowledge that every ambition is doomed to frustration at the hands of a skeleton have never prevented the majority of human beings from behaving as though death were no more than an unfounded rumour."
> —Aldous Huxley, "Variations on a Baroque Tomb," 1950

"Hell is of this world and there are men who are unhappy escapees from hell, escapees destined ETERNALLY to reenact their escape."
> —Antoine Artaud, *Selected Writings*, published in 1976

Heaven and Hell

"Hell is out of fashion—institutional hells at any rate. The populated infernos of the 20th century are more private affairs, the gaps between the bars are the sutures of one's own skull. . . . A valid hell is one from which there is a possibility of redemption, even if this is never achieved, the dungeons of an architecture of grace whose spires point to some kind of heaven. The institutional hells of the present century are reached with one-way tickets, marked Nagasaki and Buchenwald, worlds of terminal horror even more final than the grave."

—J. G. Ballard, "Visions of Hell," 1984

"Hell is a city much like London—
A populous and a smoky city;
There are all sorts of people undone,
And there is little or no fun done;
Small justice shown, and still less pity."

—Percy Bysshe Shelley, "Hell," *Peter Bell the Third*, 1819

"I myself am hell;
nobody's here—"

—Robert Lowell, "Skunk Hour," 1957

"That penny farthing hell you call your mind."

—Samuel Beckett, "Eh Joe," 1965

"I believe that I am in hell, therefore I am there."

—Arthur Rimbaud, *A Season in Hell*, 1873

"We must prefer real hell to an imaginary paradise."

—Simone Weil, "Illusions," in *Gravity and Grace*, 1947

"Ah! I have lost my freedom, and hell is now beginning."

—Albert Camus, *The Misunderstanding*, 1958

"The gates of Hell are open night and day;
Smooth the descent, and easy is the way:
But, to return, and view the cheerful skies;
In this, the task and mighty labour lies."

—Virgil, *Aeneid*, first century B.C.

Heaven and Hell

"For mortal men there is but one hell, and that is the folly and wickedness and spite of his fellows; but once his life is over, there's an end to it: his annihilation is final and entire, of him nothing survives."

—Marquis de Sade, *L'Histoire de Juliette*, 1798

"There is no dignity in wickedness, whether in purple or rags; and hell is a democracy of devils, where all are equals."

—Herman Melville, *The Writings of Herman Melville*, published in 1969

"I will go to the garden.
I will be a romantic. I will sell
myself in hell,
in heaven also I will be."

—Robert Creeley, "The Door," 1959

"War and culture, those are the two poles of Europe, her heaven and hell, her glory and shame, and they cannot be separated from one another. When one comes to an end, the other will end also and one cannot end without the other. The fact that no war has broken out in Europe for fifty years is connected in some mysterious way with the fact that for fifty years no new Picasso has appeared either."

—Milan Kundera, *Immortality*, 1988

"Dying
Is an art, like everything else.
I do it exceptionally well.
I do it so it feels like hell.
I do it so it feels real.
I guess you could say I've a call."

—Sylvia Plath, "Lady Lazarus," 1965

"If you think about it seriously, all the questions about the soul and the immortality of the soul and paradise and hell are at bottom only a way of seeing this very simple fact: that every action of ours is passed on to others according to its value, of good or evil, it passes from father to son, from one generation to the next, in a perpetual movement."

—Antonio Gramsci, *Letters from Prison*, 1933

QUOTATIONS: PURGATORY

"All know that all the dead in the world about that place are stuck
And that should mother seek her son she'd have but little luck
Because the fires of Purgatory have ate their shapes away;
I swear to God I questioned them and all they had to say
Was fol de rol de rolly O."

> —William Butler Yeats, "The Pilgrim," 1938

"Happy is the man who hath never known what it is to taste of fame—
to have it is a purgatory, to want it is a hell."

> —Edward George Earle Bulwer-Lytton,
> *Last of the Barons*, Book V, 1846

"And the frigid burnings of purgatory will not be touched
By any emollient."

> —Henry Reed, "Chard Whitlow," 1941

"Of all the inhabitants of the inferno, none but Lucifer knows that hell
is hell, and the secret function of purgatory is to make of heaven an
effective reality."

> —Arnold Bennett, *Journals*, published in 1932

PROVERBS OF HELL BY WILLIAM BLAKE
Excerpt from *The Marriage of Heaven and Hell* (1790)

In seed time learn, in harvest teach, in winter enjoy.
Drive your cart and your plow over the bones of the dead.
The road of excess leads to the palace of wisdom.
Prudence is a rich ugly old maid courted by Incapacity.
He who desires but acts not, breeds pestilence.
The cut worm forgives the plow.
Dip him in the river who loves water.
A fool sees not the same tree that a wise man sees.

Heaven and Hell

He whose face gives no light, shall never become a star.

Eternity is in love with the productions of time.

The busy bee has no time for sorrow.

The hours of folly are measur'd by the clock, but of wisdom: no clock can measure.

All wholsom food is caught without a net or a trap.

Bring out number weight & measure in a year of dearth.

No bird soars too high, if he soars with his own wings.

A dead body revenges not injuries.

The most sublime act is to set another before you.

If the fool would persist in his folly he would become wise.

Folly is the cloke of knavery.

Shame is Prides cloke.

Prisons are built with stones of Law, Brothels with bricks of Religion.

The pride of the peacock is the glory of God.

The lust of the goat is the bounty of God.

The wrath of the lion is the wisdom of God.

The nakedness of woman is the work of God.

Excess of sorrow laughs. Excess of joy weeps.

The roaring of lions, the howling of wolves, the raging of the stormy sea, and the destructive sword, are portions of eternity too great for the eye of man.

The fox condemns the trap, not himself.

Joys impregnate. Sorrows bring forth.

Let man wear the fell of the lion. woman the fleece of the sheep.

The bird a nest, the spider a web, man friendship.

The selfish smiling fool, & the sullen frowning fool shall be both thought wise, that they may be a rod.

What is now proved was once only imagin'd.

The rat, the mouse, the fox, the rabbet; watch the roots; the lion, the tyger, the horse, the elephant, watch the fruits.

The cistern contains: the fountain overflows.

One thought fills immensity.

Always be ready to speak your mind, and a base man will avoid you.

Every thing possible to be believ'd is an image of truth.

The eagle never lost so much time, as when he submitted to learn of the crow.

The fox provides for himself. but God provides for the lion.

Think in the morning. Act in the noon. Eat in the evening. Sleep in the night.

He who has suffer'd you to impose on him knows you.

As the plow follows words, so God rewards prayers.

The tygers of wrath are wiser than the horses of instruction.

Expect poison from the standing water.

You never know what is enough unless you know what is more than enough.

Listen to the fools reproach! it is a kingly title!

The eyes of fire, the nostrils of air, the mouth of water, the beard of earth.

The weak in courage is strong in cunning.

The apple tree never asks the beech how he shall grow; nor the lion, the horse, how he shall take his prey.

The thankful reciever bears a plentiful harvest.

If others had not been foolish, we should be so.

The soul of sweet delight can never be defil'd.

When thou seest an Eagle, thou seest a portion of Genius. lift up thy head!

As the catterpiller chooses the fairest leaves to lay her eggs, so the priest lays his curse on the fairest joys.

To create a little flower is the labour of ages.

Damn braces: Bless relaxes.

The best wine is the oldest, the best water the newest.

Prayers plow not! Praises reap not!

Joys laugh not! Sorrows weep not!

The head Sublime, the heart Pathos, the genitals Beauty, the hands & feet Proportion.

As the air to a bird or the sea to a fish, so is contempt to the contemptible.

The crow wish'd every thing was black, the owl, that every thing was white.

Exuberance is Beauty.

If the lion was advised by the fox. he would be cunning.

Improvement makes strait roads, but the crooked roads without
   Improvement, are roads of Genius.

Sooner murder an infant in its cradle than nurse unacted desires.

Where man is not, nature is barren.

Truth can never be told so as to be understood, and not be believ'd.

Enough! or Too much.

SAINTS—DON'T LEAVE HOME WITHOUT ONE

A saint is basically a person filled with godliness, though the term is colloquially applied to any person who is unusually patient, kind, and generous. In Islam, a saint is a *wali*. In Judaism, a *tzaddik* is a righteous person but not exactly a saint, in the sense of divine being. A patron saint is a saint who watches over a specific region or sector of the population.

THE CATHOLIC SAINT CLUB'S
CARDINAL RULES

1. You must be dead   2. You must perform two miracles

The Protocol

FIRST MIRACLE: After performing one miracle, a deceased saint "candidate" may be beatified, receiving the "blessedness" of heaven (via the pope).

SECOND MIRACLE: After two miracles or more, the deceased is included. Make sure someone sees the miracles. (If a tree falls and nobody sees or hears it, did a tree fall?)

100 VOCATIONAL SAINTS

(FYI: The saint of lost vocations is Gotteschalk)

ASTRONAUTS, Joseph of Cupertino

BEEKEEPERS, Ambrose

BIRD DEALERS, John the Baptist

BOMB TECHNICIANS, Barbara

BOOKBINDERS, Celestine V (pope), John of God

CHEFS, Lawrence, Macarius the Younger, Paschal Babylon

CIRCUS WORKERS, Julian the Hospitaller

CLOCK MAKERS, Eligius

CLOTH DYERS, Lydia Purpuraria

COFFIN MAKERS, Stephen the Martyr

CRUSADERS, Charles the Good, Louis IX

DAIRY WORKERS, Brigid of Ireland

DIPLOMATS, Gabriel the Archangel

ECOLOGISTS, Francis of Assisi

EDITORS, John Bosco, Francis de Sales

ENGINEERS, Ferdinand III of Castile, Joseph, Patrick

ENGRAVERS, John the Apostle, Thiemo

FARMERS, Isidore the Farmer

FERRYMEN, Julian the Hospitaller

FIREFIGHTERS, Florian

FISH DEALERS, Assumption of the Blessed Virgin, Apostle Andrew (and
    others)

FLORISTS, Therese of Lisieux, Rose of Lima, Bl. Rose of Viterbo

FLOUR MERCHANTS, Honorius of Amiens

FORESTERS, John Gualbert

FRUIT DEALERS, Christopher

FUNERAL DIRECTORS, Joseph of Arimathea

FURRIERS, Hubert of Liege

GARDENERS, Adelard

GAS STATION WORKERS, Eligius

GEOMETRICIANS, Apostle Thomas

GLOVE MAKERS, Crispin and Crispinian, Mary Magdalene

GOLDSMITHS, Anastasius, Eligius

GRAVE DIGGERS, Antony the Abbot

GREETING CARD MANUFACTURER, Valentine

GUARDS, Matthew the Apostle

GUNNERS, Barbara

HAIRDRESSERS, Martin de Porres, Cosmas and Damian

HARDWARE/IRON MONGERS, Sebastian

HARVESTERS, Peter the Apostle

HAYMAKERS, Gervase, Protase

HEALTH INSPECTORS, Raphael the Archangel

HORSESHOE MAKERS, Eligius, John the Baptist

HOSIERS, Fiacre

HOTELIERS, Gentian (though Italian hoteliers have their own saint, Martha)

HOUSEWIVES, Anne, Martha, Monica, Zita

INFORMATION WORKERS, Archangel Gabriel

INNKEEPERS, Gentian

JEWELERS, Eligius

JOURNALISTS, Francis de Sales

JUDGES, JURISTS, John of Capistrano, Ivo of Kermartin

JUGGLERS, Julian the Hospitaller

KNIFE GRINDERS, Catherine of Alexandria

LAMPMAKERS, Our Lady of Loreto

LAWYERS, Thomas More, Yves, Raymond of Peñafort, Ivo of Kermartin (clearly this wily group requires *many* saints)

LIGHTHOUSE KEEPERS, Venerius

LINGUISTS, Gotteschalk

MAIDS, Zita

MARINERS, Nicholas of Tolentino

MILITARY ENGINEERS, Barbara

MILLINERS, Severus of Avranches

NURSES OF THE MENTALLY ILL, Dymphna (please note: she is the same saint assigned to sleepwalkers)

OIL REFINERS, Honrius of Amiens

OLD CLOTHES DEALERS, Saint Anne

OWNERS OF COFFEEHOUSES, Drogo, Nativity of the Blessed Virgin

PARATROOPERS, Michael the Archangel

PENCIL MAKERS, Thomas Aquinas

PHARMACISTS, Cosmas and Damian

PHILOSOPHERS, Immaculate Conception of Mary

PLAYING CARD MANUFACTURERS, Balthasar

PORK BUTCHERS, transfiguration of our Lord

POSTAL WORKERS, Gabriel the Archangel

PUBLIC RELATIONS, Bernadine of Siena

RADIO WORKERS, Gabriel the Archangel

ROAD BUILDERS, Sebastian of Aparicio

ROPE MAKERS, ROPE BRAIDERS, Apostle Paul

SALESMEN, Lucy of Syracuse

SHOEMAKERS, Cyprian of Carthage

SOAP BOILERS, Florian

SPANISH CATHOLIC WRITERS, Teresa of Avila

SPELUNKERS, Benedict, Abbot (is there a living to be had in this recreational field?)

STARCH MAKERS, Charles Borromeo

STENOGRAPHERS, Cassian of Imola

STOCKBROKERS, Matthew the Apostle

SURGEONS, Cosmas and Damian, Luke, Roch

SWORDSMITHS, Maurice

TELEVISION WORKERS, Gabriel the Archangel

TENT MAKERS, Apostle Paul

TINSMITHS, Joseph of Arimathea

TRAVEL HOSTESSES, Anthony of Padua

TRUCK DRIVERS, Christopher

TRUSS MAKERS, Foillan

UPHOLSTERERS, Feast of the Immaculate Conception

VETERINARIANS, Our Lady of Coromoto

VINEGAR MAKERS, Vincent of Saragossa (this saint is working double-time, See WINE GROWERS)

WANDERING MINSTRELS AND MUSICIANS, Julian the Hospitaller

WAX MELTERS AND REFINERS, Ambrose of Milan

WINE GROWERS, Vincent of Saragossa

WINE MERCHANTS AND WINE TRADE, Amand

WOOL MANUFACTURERS, Severus of Avranches
WRITERS, Francis de Sales

SAINTS FOR THE NE'ER-DO-WELL

AGAINST THE DEVIL, Dionysus the Aeropagite
CRIMINALS, Dominic
ESCAPE FROM DEVILS, Margaret (or Marina) of Antioch
HANGOVERS, Bibiana
JUVENILE DELINQUENTS, Dominic Savio
LAWYERS, Thomas More, Yves, Raymons of Peñafort
MURDERERS, Caedwalla, Julian the Hospitaller, Nicholas of Myra, Vladimir
OPPOSITION OF CHURCH AUTHORITIES, Elizabeth Ann Seton, Joan of Arc, Teresa of Avïla
SEXUAL TEMPTATION, Angela of Foligno, Catherine of Siena, Margaret of Cortona, Mary of Edessa, Mary of Egypt, Mary Magdalene, Mary Magdalen of Pazzi, Pelagia of Antioch
SOULS IN PURGATORY, Nicholas of Tolentino, Odilo
STOCKBROKERS, Matthew the Apostle
TEENAGERS, Aloysius Gonzaga
THIEVES, Dismas, Nicholas of Myra
VENERAL DISEASE, Fiacre

CITY SAINTS

ACTORS, GENESIUS, Vitus
ACTRESSES, Pelagia
ART DEALERS, John the Apostle
ARTISTS, Luke, Catherine of Bologna
BARTENDERS, Amand
DANCERS, Vitus
EXCLUDED PEOPLE, Patrick
FEAR OF NIGHT, Giles

FEET PROBLEMS, Peter the Apostle, Servatus

HANGOVERS, Bibiana

HEADACHES, Teresa of Avila, Denis, Bishop of Paris

NEWS DEALERS, Annunciation of the Blessed Virgin

PROTECTION AGAINST MICE, Gertrude, Servatus, Ulric

PROTECTION AGAINST RATS, Gertrude of Nivelles, Martin de Porres, Servatus

PUBLIC RELATIONS, Bernadine of Siena

RABIES, Hubert, Ubald

RESTAURATEURS, Lawrence, Nicholas

TAXI DRIVERS, Fiacre

COUNTRY SAINTS

AGAINST BAD WEATHER, Eurosia, Medard

AGAINST CATERPILLARS, Magnus of Fussen

AGAINST DISEASED CATTLE, Beuno, Erhard of Regensburg, Roch, Sebastian

AGAINST INSECTS, Dominic of Silos

AGAINST MINE COLLAPSE, Barbara

FARMWORKERS, Benedict, Abbot

HAIL, Magnus of Fussen

HOGS, PIGS, SWINE, Anthony the Abbot

INSECT BITES, Mark the Apostle, Narcissus

LIVESTOCK, Isidore the Farmer

RURAL COMMUNITIES, Isidore the Farmer

SHEEP, Drogo

SICK ANIMALS, Beuno, Dwynwen, Nicholas of Tolentino

OTHER SAINTS TO KEEP IN MIND

HEMORRHOID SUFFERERS, Fiacre

INTERNET, Isidore of Seville

Heaven and Hell

LEAPING, Venantius
STAMMERING CHILDREN, Notkar Balbulus
UNATTRACTIVE PEOPLE, Drogo, Germaine Cousin

For more information on saints, refer to Father Butler's *Lives of the Saints*, first published between 1756 and 1759. In the 1956 edition, 2,565 saints were listed. A new edition is currently in progress.

SOURCES

The material for this book was extracted from hundreds of sources, ranging from reference books to Web sites, along with specialists in "the field." The books listed below are just a few of the many wonderful sources used for this project.

Dictionary of Symbolism: Cultural Icons and the Meanings behind Them, by Hans Biedermann

Egyptian Religion: Egyptian Ideas of the Future Life, by E. A. Wallis Budge

Lives of the Saints II, by Thomas J. Donaghy

New Religions, A Guide: New Religious Movements, Sects and Alternative Spiritualities, ed. Christopher Partridge

Sacred Origins of Profound Things, by Charles Panati

The Bible

The Dictionary of Imaginary Places, by Alberto Manguel and Gianni Guadalupi

The Encyclopedia of Angels, by Rosemary Ellen Guiley

The Goetia: The Lesser Key of Solomon the King, trans. Samuel Liddell and MacGregor Mathers, with an introduction by Aleister Crowley

The Religion Book: Places, Prophets, Saints, and Seers, by Jim Willis

ACKNOWLEDGMENTS

A special thanks to Richard Abate, Amy Hundley, and Brando Skyhorse. Additional thanks go to Columbia University's reference librarians, to Jennifer Emick for her fine research on alternative religions (altreligion. about.com), and to Anne Hillam, Tara Bray Smith, Lawrence Snider, Stephanie Snider, Ida Snider, Maxine Snider, and Lauren Weber, for additional research, support, and inspiration.